ತ⁀

THE HEART OF IGNATIUS

ತ THE

The Ignatian Concepts of the

HEART OF IGNATIUS

Honor and Service of God

BY PAUL DONCOEUR, S.J.

TRANSLATED BY HENRY ST. C. LAVIN, S.J.

1959

HELICON PRESS • BALTIMORE, MARYLAND

Library of Congress Catalog Card Number 59 13367

First published in France by A. L'Orante under the title *L'Honneur et Service de Dieu selon Saint Ignace de Loyola.*

This edition first published 1959

NIHIL OBSTAT: Edward A. Cerny, S. S., D. D.

IMPRIMI POTEST: Guglielmus F. Maloney, S. J.
                Praepositus Provinciae Marylandiae, S. J.
                24 Iunii 1959.

IMPRIMATUR: Most Reverend Francis P. Keough, D. D.
               Archbishop of Baltimore
               August 10, 1959

PRINTED IN THE U.S.A. BY THE NORTH CENTRAL PUBLISHING CO., ST. PAUL, MINN.

TRANSLATOR'S PREFACE

For many readers the picture of St. Ignatius Loyola which emerges from a reading of this collection of his own works will be a new and surprising one. Many of the saints have suffered from being stereotyped over the years. They have been frozen into attitudes of simpering sweetness, of hollow-cheeked gloom. Sentimental art and mistaken piety have, only too often, stripped the saints of their humanity. Yet it was only through the gradual and laborious sanctification of this humanity that they could have become saints. Only as human beings could they practice faith, hope and charity to a heroic degree; only as human beings can they provide us with guidance, norms, and inspiration.

Perhaps the image of no saint has suffered greater distortion than that of Ignatius Loyola. The metaphor which is most often associated with him is a military one. His name has come to suggest the rattling of sabres in forgotten wars, the mailed fist and stern face of military authority. To his enemies and to his admirers his name has come to suggest a kind of

Spanish-Prussianism, and he symbolizes a cult of unbending discipline and of blind obedience for its own sake. Ignatius and the Society of Jesus which he founded have come, in the eyes of many, to stand for a spiritual ethos of cold efficiency, without warmth, without joy, without heart.

This translation is entitled *The Heart of Ignatius* in an attempt to suggest that this picture of Ignatius is at very best partial and incomplete. No one who reads Father Doncoeur's selections from the writings of St. Ignatius can miss the fact that the traditional picture oversimplifies a complex character and omits some of the most basic aspects of it. The most important thing, of course, is not authority, but love. The love of Ignatius was Catholic and catholic. It was love which inspired his conversion and his penances. When once he had glimpsed the majesty and the beauty of God, his response was a wholehearted love which made every sacrifice seem small. Love drove him to the Holy Land to follow the footsteps of Christ; love brought him back again to find Christ everywhere and in everyone. It was love which inspired what was perhaps the greatest penance of his life, his return to the classroom to prepare himself, among little boys, for the work which he would do for God.

His love was not a matter of barren words. All his life he distrusted fluent professions and looked, in himself and in others, for a love which shows itself in deeds. So, love for the Church of Christ meant "thinking with the Church." It meant working with and for the Church in foreign missions, in missions to the faithful, in universities, and in teaching catechism to children. He had no favorite work; he had only a motive for working, the honor and glory of the God he loved.

He found God in his Jesuit sons, in sinners, in nature itself. In a kind of circular movement his love of God led him to people and to things, and these in turn led him back to God. His was a unified vision of life, clear and undistracted. For him there were not two loves, but one. Not to see Ignatius as a man in love is to miss the central theme which gives his life and his work meaning.

To see Ignatius as an unbending disciplinarian is to forget his faith in the power of the Holy Spirit. He knew well that those who attempt to lead a spiritual life in a religious order or out of it need a stabilizing framework of rules and practices to regulate the vagaries of emotion and unify the fragments of an active life. But he realized even more that to rely on these alone is to fall. In his *Spiritual Exercises* and in the *Constitutions* which he wrote for his Society it is "the interior law of charity and love, which the Holy Spirit is accustomed to imprint in the hearts of men," on which he relied. A mystic himself, he placed no limits on the spiritual aspirations of his followers, save the traditional ones of prudence and orthodoxy. And in practical matters of government, he left great freedom to Provincials and to local superiors. He was no authoritarian dictator who feared freedom. Within the broad framework of rule, he hoped that the love of God and the inspiration of the Holy Spirit would lead men to the heights.

The ethos of Ignatius which he tried to communicate to his followers was one of total devotion, devotion to God and to the Son of God, to our Lady and the Church, and to the children of God everywhere. Such devotion, he knew, would lead ultimately to success, though the way might be the way of the Cross and the success perceptible only to the vision of faith. He advocated the choice of the Christlike thing in every situation, knowing that this would often seem foolishness and be a stumbling block. For him, to love Christ was to follow Christ, and to follow Christ was to choose what Christ had chosen: poverty, contempt, and the Cross. This was no spiritual masochism but a love which wished to follow the Beloved by obedience and imitation.

A heart, like a heart of Ignatius, in love with God, rejects only sin; having rejected sin, it is then free to reach out to the world, God's world, with love expressed in devotion.

Something like this is the picture of St. Ignatius which emerges from Father Doncoeur's book. It is filled in by the words of St. Ignatius himself and by the understanding and sympathetic commentary of Father Doncoeur. It is not a biography; there are a number of excellent biographies of

St. Ignatius. It is not a book of meditations, but it is a meditative book. It takes time to form a saint, and it takes time to know one. St. Ignatius is worth knowing, not merely because of his historical importance, but because he loved God and because he would speak to us of the love of God. This is the message of Christianity; it is the message of all the saints; it is the message of Ignatius Loyola. It is the heart of Ignatius.

My thanks are due to Edward A. Ryan and Elmer O'Brien, both priests of the Society of Jesus, for their encouragement and help during the course of this translation.

I dedicate this work to my mother and father.

July 31, 1959   Henry St. C. Lavin, S.J.

CONTENTS

INTRODUCTION

St. Ignatius has left us neither treatise, nor sermons, nor any personal documents which formulate a systematic spiritual teaching. The fragments of his Journal are but cries of the heart, pleadings and tears. His immense correspondence is that of a chief of staff, governing an army of apostles who are engaged in all the spiritual battles of their era. We find some few letters of spiritual doctrine, but many of these betray the hands of the secretaries to whom Ignatius entrusted the task of expressing his thought. The Autobiography, in which the story of the first years of his conversion is movingly told, is far from doctrinal in aim and scope. What then remains? The Spiritual Exercises, his masterpiece, and the Constitutions of the Society of Jesus, designed as they are to be guides and handbooks for action, are not in literary form. In line with their practical purpose, they are but terse statements which never are elaborated into theoretical speculations.

Although he was able to find short and pregnant expressions, fitted for expressing a word of command, Ignatius rarely achieved that felicity of phrase which lends charm even to the driest texts written by a man of genius. He lacked brilliance of expression, clarity and allusiveness of phrase, and, still more, spontaneity of imagery and feeling. Language failed him; and there are many reasons for this.

God had not given him the gift. From his race he inherited great natural endowments, but the Basques are not a literary people. This knight, reader of tales of romance, never attained scholastic excellence. And his roving career, which took him out of his normal environment, forced upon him an unnatural state of uprootedness.

His native language was Basque. We do not know how well he used it. As a young page he spoke Castilian, which became his customary language, but remained practically a foreign tongue to him.* We know what difficulties he had when, at thirty, he began spelling out the elements of Latin. Later, at Paris and at Rome, he had to speak French and Italian. There was never time to make himself master of any language; and in all probability he had neither facility nor taste for such study.

One of his first companions, Father James Lainez, said afterward that his preaching did not follow the canons of Cicero or of Quintilian, but that it was more effective than any studied rhetoric. "A thing," Ignatius said, "has only that value which God puts upon it; and He usually values it insofar as it is united to Him for good work, as a tool in a worker's hand." [1]

We know from many sources that his speech, which was jejune by the world's standards, became, in God's hands, a triumphant power. It kept the novelty-seekers away, while it attracted souls eager for God. This is a sufficient gift.

One of his youngest novices, who later became his confidant and his biographer, gives us a significant example of this. Peter Ribadeneira relates:

* The Monumenta Ignatiana, in the volume on the Exercises contains a study of St. Ignatius' improper usages in Castilian vocabulary and grammar. An article in the Revue des Études Basques (1936), p. 53–61, points out the numerous irregularities of syntax (frequent use of the gerundive, infinitives used substantively, etc.) which are "Basquisms."

"Since our Father was not eloquent, but unskilled in speech, and especially since he had studied the Italian language but little, I, though only a boy, admonished this holy old man that there were many mistakes in his speech, many things which should be corrected because he gave them Spanish rather than Italian forms. 'Good!' he said, 'take note if any mistakes occur and correct me.' So the next day I began to observe our Father while he spoke, and to note down in writing any foreign words, incorrect pronunciations, and so on, in order not to forget them. But when I saw that not one or other word, but the whole sermon would have to be changed, I despaired of any improvement and stopped taking notes and told our Father what had happened. Then he said, 'Well, Peter, what shall we do for God?' This is all the more wonderful since at that time I was a boy of scarcely fourteen years.

"But," *Ribadeneira continues,* "I recall that one day he concluded a sermon by saying, *'Amar a Dio, con todo el core, con toda l'anima, con toda la voluntad . . .'* (a mixture of Spanish and Italian), but saying it with such force and fervor that his countenance seemed to glow. And sinners afterward flocked to confession. And Fr. Lainez has often spoken of this incident." *

It is that accent of deep feeling which made an impression. We can imagine the accent of St. Francis of Assisi, who merely by repeating the name of Jesus set the heart of St. Clare aflame. We know the accent of the Curé of Ars. We can imagine that of St. Paul, bearing witness to Christ at Ephesus or Corinth. If we seek an analogue for the incorrect and ungrammatical prose of Ignatius, we will find it in Paul's Epistles. They both speak with the same lack of art and the same fire of love. It is that fire which I have tried to transfer to these pages. But in an inadequate translation we can only gather its almost extinguished embers.

When we have copied from the works of this genius even those pages in which his talent seems to reach its full development, we shall be in error if we think that we have ade-

---

* *M.I. Script.*, I, p. 358, # 47.

quately caught and transmitted his thought. The thought of such a man is inseparable from his action. The work of such a man is not literary but living. Perhaps we shall perceive that we were wrong in believing that the greatest spiritual masters were writers. Rather they were messengers, prophets, patriarchs. From Jean-Marie Vianney to Francis of Assisi, from Dominic to John the Baptist, the most influential guides of souls have been those most like their Master. And He certainly was not a writer of books.

St. Ignatius is of this lineage. His thought and teaching are inseparably linked to his plan of action. It is in the by-way of a note, in the incidental remarks of a conversation, and, as it were, in the flash of an avowal of love that we must catch them. But the desire to gather together these breaths of the Spirit seems futile, as futile as the game which children play when they try to carry home with them the glimmering fires of a phosphorescent sea.

We must live with a saint like Ignatius; patiently we must catch the rhythm of his activity, enter into his thought and absorb it. Then, after years of fervent study, the inner grandeur of his holiness may be revealed. Not as listeners, not as students, but as sons shall we, by a vital communion, at last understand the thoughts which could only bewilder the curious.

St. Ignatius is ordinarily spoken of with respect, although many find even this difficult. How rarely do people speak of him with love! So consistently does he attack the spirit of the world, that the world has chosen to leave him severely alone. A great many name their children Dominic, or Bruno, Francis, or Benedict. But how few are willing to acknowledge such trusting intimacy with St. Ignatius?

Only those who have had the courage to mold their lives according to his word will at times be able to taste its force and meaningfulness. If some soul by dint of prayer finds in his word an impulse to love, it will have shown the truth of that thought so dear to St. Ignatius, "For it is not to know much, but it is to understand and savor the matter interiorly that fills and satisfies the soul (*gustare et sentire res in-*

terne)." * *Words of such power and inspiration show that St. Ignatius is far more than a teacher. He is a master of our souls. "Tu verba vitae habes."*

We have tried here to copy out a few of these words of life. Snatched from their context, while still alive with the inspiration that created them, they should have been inserted in a fabric which would reveal the vital harmony of the thought behind them. They were addressed to particular individuals in definite circumstances. They sped from one soul to another. Perhaps it would have been enough to retain the overtones of familiar speech. Still the only way to be faithful and intelligible would have been to maintain the close connection between word and action, between thought and man and, if possible, between God and this messenger. Almost the whole life of St. Ignatius would have had to be retold to support the citations which have gone into this little book. At least I have tried to keep clearly in mind the image of the saint and the outlines of his work. I could not present Ignatius' teaching as separable from the men to whom it was addressed, nor as distinct from the Society whose life is the concrete embodiment of that doctrine. The thoughts of an artist, the cosmic vision of a poet are better expressed in their art than in their theories. So the thoughts of Ignatius on man, the world and God are nowhere better expressed than in the imposing and solid structure of the Society of Jesus which is so much more complex and true than any synthesis of thought. For time and persecutions have tried and proved its strength.

Others may seem more subtle or more profound, more logical or wise. But he surpasses all the theorists who can offer us a product which has been tried by changes of place and circumstance and not found wanting. Such a work bears with it proof of the genius which conceived and built it. It is signed with the mark of God without which human works are merely specious and feeble. It is not hard to see why contemporaries misunderstood it, for the plan was original, bold, and occasionally even revolutionary. But after four

* *Exercises,* 2.

centuries, it is futile to waste time in argument when it is so easy to open one's eyes and see the living work.

This organic bond between work and word explains why the thought of Ignatius has a character which is rare among teachers. Those who write are, in general, influenced by a logical sequence of ideas. Possessed of a limited view of things, they express it with truth and force. They write dissertations. One will give the world a philosophy of contingent being and exalt the transcendence of the Creator. Another will make flow into the hearts of men that divine peace which is the result of a complete dedication to His love. Another will kindle hearts at the fire of Christ's Passion. Another will hymn poverty, still another announce the coming of the kingdom.

The better we know him, the more we wonder at the harmonies of the heart of Ignatius. Joined there are traits which we would have thought incompatible. His stoical Principle and Foundation reminds us of the noblest pages of Epictetus and the wisdom of Pythagoras. When he leads us to contemplate scenes from the life of Christ, he has Bonaventure's tenderness. His love for his crucified Lord is as passionate as that of Francis of Assisi. He analyzes the movements of the soul under the influence of good and evil spirits with the subtlety of St. Francis de Sales. He loses himself with the philosophical mystics in the contemplation of the Supreme Unity. He spans the world and traces on the oceans a path for the Gospel with the same care as explorers who have felt the fascination of the East. An ardent thirst for poverty consumes him and he spends tense weeks impressing the seal of poverty on the rules of his Society. He exalts obedience as the characteristic virtue of his sons, but he then proclaims that the law of charity and love, which is written by the Holy Spirit on the hearts of men, is their supreme rule. He makes his order the light cavalry of the Church, vowed soul and body to the pope, but he devotes it also to the spiritual service of princes. He demands from his sons skill in science and letters while protesting that only union with God makes them effective instruments.

From this diversity of thought and conduct we could draw spiritual systems so divergent that their coexistence would seem irreconcilable in a wise and orderly mind. Rather we must give up the attempt to fit him into the framework of any school. Men have called him the rigid theorist of asceticism, when he is quite as much the herald of love and the master of contemplation. They have said that he was anthropocentric, although his ruling passion is for the glory of God. It would be easy to multiply the contrasts which amaze the geometricians and disturb the logicians of the spiritual life. In like manner we can find all the rules of wisdom in his work because, being a realist, he refused to adopt the deceptive or dangerously widespread oversimplifications of visionaries. By the same token he is a prudent guide according to the word of God: "a scribe instructed in the Kingdom of Heaven who brings forth from his storeroom things new and old" *(cf. Mt. 13:52). For four centuries he has imparted to souls as diverse as Xavier, Alphonsus Rodríguez, Stanislaus, Bellarmine, Faber and Borgia, that varied grace which is the reflection of the infinite richness of God. From men as impetuous as himself he required discipline capable of transforming into docile labor their otherwise explosive forces. For the less zealous he has the spur they need. A thoroughbred must be held in check, oxen must be yoked and goaded. In this way he drew from all their greatest efforts for the greater glory of God.*

Ignatius discovered in his own soul the science of men and the secret of the ways of God. The Exercises are the story of his conversion from the world to God. All that he has written there is the fruit of his own experience.

Humbly he acknowledged his debt to the Spirit of God, the interior Master who taught him more than he learned by his own efforts or by close attention to the teachers of his time. St. Paul often referred to the things he had learned not from the apostles, but from Christ Himself. When he does this, his words take on an accent, at once direct and free, humble and proud, which is unmistakable. In this little book we have tried to gather from the writings of Ignatius

*that which is spontaneous; that which directly expresses his
vital, personal ideas; that which is from God. This it is, no
doubt, which will be best understood by the uninitiated
reader provided he is willing to listen to the word of God
even though the style be pedestrian. This warning would
have been given by Ignatius himself to the readers of this
book.*

To James Cazador, archdeacon of Barcelona, who had
written of his desire to see Ignatius preach in that city, he
replied:

Certainly I myself have the same desire. Not that I feel
any pride in doing a thing which others cannot do, nor in
reaching a place that others cannot reach. But I would wish
to preach, like an ordinary man, of things that are simple
and easy to understand, hoping in God our Lord, that by
following this ordinary way His grace will enable us to
achieve something for His glory and the service which is
due to Him.[2]   *Venice, February 12, 1536*

*This book is not written for historians, nor for experts in
spirituality. Still less will those who are familiar with all the
teachings of St. Ignatius because of long contact with the
Spiritual Exercises or the Constitutions find new light in it.
But the ordinary reader is often frightened, perhaps, by an
esoteric manner of presentation in which the reasoning and
the language suppose previous preparation. The Exercises
remain virtually a closed book except to those whom a living
commentator has initiated to an otherwise unfamiliar doctrine and vocabulary.* *

*For this reason we have tried to embody the thought of
Ignatius in very ordinary language which will be easily
understood by all. The reader should seek in these pages
only a first initiation.*

*This care, however, has not prevented us from pointing
to the far horizons to which the genius and sanctity of Igna-*

---

* *Thus the "Annotations," or the "Additions," not to mention the "Composition of Place," or the "Colloquies;" but explanation is still more necessary
to clarify the meaning of the "three degrees of humility," the "three classes,"
etc. It is asserted in the Society that one does not read the Exercises, but
makes them under the direction of a man versed in their practice.*

18

tius direct us. We hope that they may appear the more clearly by being freed from all which might distract the gaze.

This far horizon is marked by two peaks. On one side rises Ignatius' burning zeal for the honor of God, on the other his ardent love of Jesus Christ.

By nature Ignatius was of a passionate temperament. And when he had once realized the sovereign majesty of God, he transferred to, and expanded in the service of the King of kings all the generous chivalry which his Spanish soul had once given to his prince. For his prince he had thrown himself, at the risk of his life, into the thick of the battle. He fell fighting bravely, only to find himself illumined by a splendor far brighter than any military glory. He arose a prouder champion in the service of a nobler Master. The Honor of God! *We can imagine his tone as he pronounced these words. All the rest of his life he burned with such zeal that no conquistador ever longed for the Indies with greater desire than he longed for the honor of God. How could he refuse to do for his God what so many soldiers and adventurers were doing for their king?*

Ignatius had the spirit of a nobleman. He could not endure lack of will power or even that mediocrity which disgraces the worldly Christian. Once he had sworn fealty to God, he cast aside all timidity in the face of infidels and rejected that calculating spirit which limits its services to what is strictly necessary. In the proud spirit of chivalry he rejects all compromises and concessions which detract from the gift. Miles ignavus, cowardly soldier, he calls the knight who hesitates or measures his response to the appeal of his Lord.

In an age of Christianity without pride in its dignity, when religion made concessions and was by turn sentimental and timeserving, Ignatius expressed the protest of a Christian who has finally understood the demands of the faith because he has glimpsed the grandeur of God.

On the other hand he had fathomed the inconceivable humility of Jesus Christ, first in His poverty, then in His

19

Passion. The heart of Ignatius could not resist. Here we see a marvelous counterpart of Franciscan tenderness. He takes on the manner of another race, of another time, of another type of man. His response to these motives for love is the complete and generous following of his King, even in the most bloody struggles. This vain and glittering captain will make himself a beggar for love of the poor Christ. Later on he will teach his Society forms of abnegation which, though less poetic, are no less demanding. He too will wage war on the spirit of the world, but in a severely disciplined manner. Modern tactics and arms render spiritual warfare less of an adventure, but not less dangerous.

Unless you have read his magnificent Journal which resounds with the cries, the sobs, the passionate prayers of a soul sometimes distraught, you will never be able to conceive how fiercely the fire burned in his heart. Unless you appreciate the violent struggles to which his racial temperament exposed him, you will have difficulty in understanding his apparently stern demands. Unless you have arrived at intimacy with him, you will never suspect that he can be a tender friend and father, capable of humble compassion and boundless patience. It would be a great mistake to consider his strictness austere coldness, his victorious enthusiasm calculating rigor. It would be a mistake to see in his counsels, which throb with emotion and love, only the orders of a master to which the disciple must conform despite himself. If you read his heart in a spirit of love, you will see that Ignatius seeks constantly the full perfection of each one according to God's will. He will not stand for pettiness; only the glory of God satisfies him. He judges nothing worthy of his ambition but the court of the greatest of kings; there only is he at ease. He can be content nowhere else. None of his sons may stop half way. Love of life, passionate love, draws him on. His words are on fire, aflame with restrained passion; but how tenderly, respectfully, wisely he guides the souls of others! If every word of Ignatius is not understood truly, is not full of the spirit which was his inspiration, you will find in him only arid and sterile formulas.

We have deliberately avoided lengthening this collection of texts and fragments, but we hope that they will bear witness to the fundamental ideas of St. Ignatius. The concepts, "Honor and Service," express the dominant themes of his heart and the purpose of all his teaching.*

It is well known that the formula, Ad maiorem Dei gloriam, which recurs so often in his writings, has become the motto of the Society of Jesus. In obedience to the Holy Father and in the teaching of children, in patient endurance of suffering and in giving counsel to princes, the sole motive which he proposes is the glory of God, "To render more honor to God."

We could have gathered testimony to this fact from all his teaching. But it will be felt that this thought is everywhere vitally present. That is why we have not made it the subject of a special chapter. For it dominates all of them.

Moreover the very name which God has given to Ignatius' company bears sufficient witness that the person of Christ is the living center of his entire life and of all his actions. The Exercises, when the necessary purification has been completed, are simply a contemplation of the person of Christ and a heartfelt offering to follow Him in perfect imitation of His poverty and sufferings. "An interior knowledge of our Lord that I may the more love Him and follow Him"—*this is the essential grace for which he wants his followers to long. And it is this grace which will animate all the attempts at personal sanctity and apostolic zeal in which he engages. This love of Christ's person is also so present in all of Ignatius' thought that it was impossible to give it a separate chapter. For it too dominates and vivifies all of them. The glory and the honor of God, the love and the service of Jesus Christ rule all his thought and all his action.*

* [An Essay on Sources appears below, p. 119 ff. — Trans.]

THE HEART OF IGNATIUS

THE HEART OF IGNATIUS

We find the source of the thought and the lifework of St. Ignatius in his boundless love for his Lord and God:

God, our Lord, who loves me more than I love myself.[3]

All his enlightenment he received from that love.

He said of his long prayer and many visions at Manresa to Fr. Gonzáles that they:

Gave him such a great and lasting strengthening of faith that even if there were no Scripture to teach him these things of faith, he would be ready to die for the faith merely because of what he had seen at that time. . . . These illuminations were so great that all these things seemed new to him, and he received such insights and was so enlightened that he felt himself almost a new man.[4]

Later these visions were less frequent, but he tells us that:

The longer he lived, the more he had of light, of strength and constancy in things divine.[5]

His Journal tells us how deeply, when he was working

25

on the revision of the Constitutions, *his thoughts and his decisions were influenced by an extraordinary motion of divine grace which filled him with love:*

A flood of tears, of sobs with such an intense love that it seemed to unite me beyond my powers to the love [of the Trinity], so luminous was it and so sweet.

I received from the Giver of graces such an abundance of divine lights that every time I spoke the name of God or of our Lord I was completely filled with a respect, a wonderful reverence and humility which seem inexpressible to me.[6]

I could not live without that divine consolation. I could not live if I did not feel in my soul something, not of me, nor in my power, not in the power of any man, but which is purely of God.[7]

From that love comes his courage. The desire for death burned within him and he found his comfort in the hope that death would come soon. At Manresa, when he was worn out with his penances, the voice of the tempter whispered to him:

"How will you be able to bear this life since you have seventy more years to live?"

He replied:

"Can you, wretched one, promise me one hour of life?"[8]

He notes in his Journal:

A great love of our Lord Jesus Christ, a very real desire to die with Him.[9]

Often he repeats:

How ugly the earth is when I gaze upon heaven![10]

When people spoke of what they would do during the next five or eight days, he would say to them:

Is that so? Are you sure that you are going to live that long?[11]

Meantime, despite his burning desire for heaven, he was carried away by zeal for the service of God, for His glory and for the salvation of souls.

One day in July, 1541, Lainez, Oviedo and Ribadeneira were chatting with him about a sermon which they had just heard.

"Master Lainez," *said Ignatius,* "if God were to say to you: 'If you want to die at once, I will give you eternal glory; but if you choose to live, I do not guarantee you the gift of final perseverance'; if you thought that by remaining on earth, you would be able to achieve some great thing, what would your choice be?"

"To die at once," *said Lainez,* "so that I would be sure."

Ignatius replied, "For my part, I wouldn't. If I thought that by continuing to live I could accomplish some great work for God, I would beg Him to leave me on earth till I had done it. I would turn my eyes toward Him and not toward myself. I would take no account of my danger, or my security." [12]

Lord, what do I desire, what could I desire, but You? *was his familiar ejaculation.* [13]

His life was a constant striving, dominated by this sole desire. Fr. Polanco reports that one day when they were on the point of leaving for Naples, he insisted that the saint put off his departure for the sake of his health because the weather was bad.

No, *Ignatius replied,* for the past thirty years no circumstance has made me omit anything which I thought I should do for the service of God. [14]

In June, 1532, he wrote from Paris to his brother, Don Martin de Oñaz:

Yes, it is true. I can love a person in this life only as much as it helps to the service and glory of God.

I greatly desire, and more than greatly, if I may say so, that in yourself, in your relations and friends there should be an abundance of this true love, and increased strength in the service and praise of God our Lord, for that would make me love you more and more. For service of the servants of my Lord is my victory and my glory. [15]

On August 10, 1546, he wrote to a friend, Doimo Narcio, who had reported to him the incendiary proposals of a zealot:

Tell Father Barbazan that if, as he says, he is so eager to have all the members of our Company, from Perpignan to Seville, burned alive, I for my part desire that all his friends,

27

not only from Perpignan to Seville, but in the whole world, may be so inflamed and enkindled by the fire of the Holy Spirit that they may all grow toward perfection to the glory of His divine Majesty.[16]

Such a love gave him not only courage, but joy. To those who expressed pity for his imprisonment at Salamanca, he said:

You do not show me love; rather you wish to steal my delights from me. If you knew what happiness it is to suffer for Christ, you would not pity, but envy me." [17]

Later he wrote to John III, king of Portugal:

After my return from Jerusalem, the authorities tried me three times at Alcalá de Henares, I was arrested and put in prison. At Salamanca after another trial, I was not only put in prison, but in chains for twenty-two days. At Paris . . . another trial. During these five trials and two imprisonments, by God's grace, I never took, nor wished to take any other lawyer or procurator than God in whom, by His grace and favor, I placed all my hopes for the present and the future. Even after this trial at Paris, seven years later there was another in the same university, then one at Venice, and the last one at Rome against the entire Society. By God's merciful grace in none of these eight trials was a single proposition, not even a syllable condemned, and I was never punished or banished. . . . People in Spain were amazed that I who had not studied spoke so much about spiritual matters. Nevertheless it is true — God, my Creator and Judge is my witness — that even to gain all temporal riches and power, I do not wish that all this had not happened. I am willing that even worse should happen to me for the greater glory of His divine Majesty.[18]

At the end of his life he could say from experience:

There is no created thing that can give greater joy to the soul or even joy equal to that which the soul receives for having suffered for Christ.[19]

It is not less a miracle to see a religious sad and troubled than to see a man who seeks everything except God joyful.[20]

Those who lived with him said:

Father Ignatius has a completely happy heart.[21]
The motif of this heart can be summed up in a phrase:
To prefer the glory of the Lord to all things.[22]

        Barcelona, December 6, 1525. To Ines Pascual.

ह्ल

PART I: THE EXERCISES

St. Ignatius sought that "glory of the Lord" with ardor through difficult paths which were thick with snares. In order to lead others through the midst of these dangers he wrote from the wealth of his own experience the book which he called:

Spiritual Exercises to conquer oneself and regulates one's life, and to avoid coming to a determination through any inordinate affection.   *Ex. p. 11; 1.* *

As to go for a walk or a journey, and to run, are bodily exercises, so is the name of spiritual exercises applied to any method of preparing and disposing the soul to free itself from all inordinate affections, and after it has freed itself from them, to seek and find the will of God concerning the ordering of life for the salvation of one's soul.   *Ex. p. 1; 1.*

* [*The quotations from the* Exercises *are based on the translation by John Morris, S.J., originally published in London in 1880 (latest printing: West-minster, Md., 1943). Therefore, the first element of the citation refers to this translation; the second figure is the marginal number assigned to the quoted section in the Spanish-Latin edition prepared by the redactor of the critical edition and published in Turin in 1928. — Trans.*]

31

It will much benefit him who is receiving the Exercises to enter upon them with a large heart and with liberality toward his Creator and Lord, offering all his desires and liberty to Him in order that His divine Majesty may make use of his person and of all that he possesses according to His most holy will. *Ex. p. 3; 5.*

The exercises which St. Ignatius gives for a retreat of four weeks are what we properly call Spiritual Exercises, but the effect of their training extends unobtrusively to one's whole life:

I consider in our Lord that if at one time we have need of such and such spiritual and physical exercises, at another we have just as much need of different exercises, and that those which have once been useful to us, are not always so later.[23] *Rome, September 20, 1548. To the Duke of Gandia.*

The scholastics can endeavor to seek the presence of our Lord in all things, in conversation with others, in walking, in looking, in tasting, in hearing, in understanding and in all that we do, since it is a fact that His divine Majesty is everywhere by presence, power and essence.[24]

Rome, June 1, 1551. To Antonio Brandano.

All these endeavors, whatever they be, seek but one object:

Above all I want you to increase the pure love of Jesus Christ in the desire of His glory and the salvation of the souls which He has redeemed.[25]

Rome, May 7, 1547. To the Scholastics at Coimbra.

After having himself lived according to the Exercises and having induced so many other souls to direct their lives by them, he wrote to a friend:

I beg you for His love and for the most cruel death which He suffered for us to saturate yourself with the *Exercises* . . . for they contain what I can conceive, feel and understand to be best in this life, so that a man may be able to benefit himself and to gather fruit to help and benefit many others.[26] *Venice, November 16, 1536. To Dr. E. de Miona.*

Chapter I THE PRINCIPLE AND FOUNDATION

The *Exercises* are built on this foundation:

Man was created to praise, reverence and serve God our Lord, and by this means to save his soul.

The other things on the face of the earth were created for man's sake, and in order to aid him in the prosecution of that end for which he was created. Whence it follows, that man must make use of them insofar as they help him to attain his end, and in the same way he ought to withdraw himself from them insofar as they hinder him from it.

It is therefore necessary that we should make ourselves indifferent to all created things, insofar as it is left to the liberty of our free will to do so, and is not forbidden; in such sort that we do not for our part wish for health rather than sickness, for wealth rather than poverty, for honor rather than dishonor, for a long life rather than a short one; and so in all other things, desiring and choosing only those which most lead us to the end for which we were created.

Ex. p. 12; 23.

All the work of God is designed to conduct the creature to that end. But unfortunately:

There are very few men who realize what God would make of them if they abandoned themselves entirely to His hands, and let themselves be formed by His grace. A thick and shapeless tree trunk would never believe that it could become a statue, admired as a miracle of sculpture . . . and would never consent to submit itself to the chisel of the sculptor who, as St. Augustine says, sees by his genius what he can make of it. Many people who, we see, now scarcely live as Christians, do not understand that they could become saints, if they would let themselves be formed by the grace of God, if they did not ruin His plans by resisting the work which He wants to do.[27]

That fundamental truth rules the judgments which we should make about things of this earth:

In this life a thing is good only in the degree in which it serves eternal life. And it is evil in that degree in which it makes us turn aside or away from it. In this way the soul, suffering contradictions on this earth, enlightened and purified by the eternal dew, builds its nest on the heights, concentrates all its desires on the search for Christ crucified since, after being crucified in this life, it will rise to life with Him in the next.[28] *Rome, April 25, 1543. To Ascanio Colonna.*

Happy are those who prepare themselves in this life to be judged and saved by His divine Majesty. For His love and respect I ask that without delay you most diligently reform your consciences so that on the day of our final and awesome destiny your souls will be confident.[29]

Rome, February 2, 1539.
To his brothers, D. Martin Garcia and D. Bertrand de Loyola.

For in reality:

Neither among men, nor among angels is there a more noble activity than to glorify your Creator, and to lead to Him as many other creatures as you can.[30]

May 7, 1547. To the scholastics at Coimbra.

Chapter II TO DIE TO SIN

In June, 1532, Ignatius wrote to his brother, Don Martin de Oñaz:

In the beginning [that is, in his sinful youth] I resembled St. Paul. For the middle and end of my life, may it please the sovereign Bounty not to refuse me all His most holy grace so that I may resemble all those who have been His true servants. And if I am ever about to offend Him, or relax in anything which relates to His holy service and praise, may that Bounty take me from this life before that happens.[31]

His greatest endeavor was to make a sincere change of life. This explains the terrible penances of those first years. All his life he kept a vivid feeling of his own unworthiness.

In ecstasy he was heard to cry out:

O God, God infinitely good, how do you bear with a sinner such as I am?[32]

I could never persuade myself that these two things are so combined in any other man as in myself — on my part to have sinned so much, and on God's part to have received so many blessings from Him.[33]

I have never treated of the things of God with a great sinner without finding him better than myself, and without having gained much good from him for my soul.[34]

He said that:

Realizing how often he had sinned and offended our Lord, he had often wished that the divine Majesty might take away from him such abundant consolations to punish him for his faults . . . but that, so great was the mercy and gentleness of our Lord in his regard, that it seemed that the more he sinned, the more he understood his sins and desired to expiate them, so much the more did our Lord give Himself to him and open to him the treasure of His consolations and gifts.[35]

May it please our Lady, *he wrote to Ines Pascual*, to stand between us, poor sinners, and her Son and Lord. May she obtain for us the grace that in the midst of our sorrows and trials, she may make our cowardly and sad spirits strong and joyous to praise Him.[36]   *December 6, 1524.*

So all the effort of the spiritual life should be to conform to the action of God, to deliver ourselves from the rule of sin, even of light faults, for:

The contempt of small faults is often more dangerous than contempt of important faults. When we commit the latter, shame accuses them automatically and they are noticed at once. Not so with the others: we do not realize the harm they do till long after.[37]

Penance is a necessary instrument for purification. In the Exercises Ignatius assigns to it three objects:

Exterior penances are used chiefly for three purposes: first as a satisfaction for past sins; secondly in order to overcome oneself, that is to say, in order that sensuality may be obedient to reason, and all that is inferior be more subjected to the superior; thirdly in order to seek and find some grace or gift which a person wishes and desires; as, for example, if he desires to have an interior sorrow for his sins, or to weep much for them, or for the pains and sufferings which Christ our Lord endured in His Passion; or in order to obtain the solution of some doubt he is in.   *Ex. p. 31; 87.*

In public necessities or for our own personal good, to obtain some favor from God, let us afflict ourselves in His eyes, praying and watching, according to the ancient custom of the saints, in sackcloth and fasting.[38]

Nevertheless:

We must apply ourselves more fervently in conquering the interior man than the body, in breaking the rebellion of the soul more than the bones.[39]

If discretion seems to you to be a rare bird and hard to capture, at least supply its lack by obedience, whose counsel is safe.

In order, then, to keep the mean between lukewarmness and indiscreet fervor, you must pay great attention to obedience, by submitting your judgment to your superiors.

If you have a strong desire to mortify yourselves during your studies, gratify it by breaking your will, by submitting your judgment to your superiors, rather than by weakening your bodies with undue severity.

Yet I would not have you conclude from this that I am displeased, or at all disapprove of what has been written me on the subject of some of the mortifications practiced among you. For these and other holy follies, I well know, have been used by the saints with great profit to their souls. They help one in the work of self-conquest, and progress in virtue, especially in the beginning of one's change of life. But when with God's grace you have gained some mastery over self-love, it is better, I take it, that you follow out what I have said in this letter on the necessity of discretion. Let obedience, then, which I so much recommend, be your rule of action; let charity, the embodiment of all virtues, reign in your hearts; for charity is God's own commandment: "This is my commandment, that you love one another as I have loved you," (Jo. 15:12).[40]

May 7, 1547. To the scholastics at Coimbra.

St. Ignatius wrote to Francis Borgia, duke of Gandia, who had been recently converted, and who was hurling himself into excessive penances:

With regard to fasting and abstinence, I would advise you

37

for the love of God to guard and fortify your stomach and your other natural forces, and not to weaken them. For when the soul is disposed and firmly determined to die rather than commit the least deliberate offense against the divine Majesty, and when besides it is not harassed by any particular temptation of the enemy, the world and the flesh, mortification is no longer so necessary. . . . I greatly desire that Your Lordship will imprint this truth on your soul: both soul and body belong to their Creator and Lord, Your Lordship will have to render an account of both of them. Therefore you should not let the body grow weak, since if it is in a weakened condition, the soul can no longer fulfill her functions . . . because we should care for the body and love it in proportion as it obeys and serves the soul more perfectly. On its part the soul finds in this obedient aid of the body more force and energy to serve and glorify our Creator and Lord.

. . . With regard to the chastisement of the body, instead of trying to shed a drop of blood, rather seek our Lord more closely in all things, I mean His holiest gifts: intensity of faith, hope and charity, joy and spiritual repose, tears and intense consolation, elevation of the spirit, divine illuminations and impressions, and all the other spiritual sweetness and feeling which flows from such gifts, as for example, humility and profound respect for our mother, holy Church, for her rulers and teachers. Of all these holy gifts, there is not one which should not be preferred to all bodily acts which are only good when they have for their aim the acquisition of these graces. I don't mean to say that we should seek them only for the satisfaction and pleasure which we find in them; but we recognize that without these gifts, all our thoughts, words and actions are confused, cold and troubled instead of being fervent, clear and fitting, for the greater service of God.

. . . So, when the body finds herself in danger as a result of laborious exercises, the best thing is to seek these gifts by mental acts, or by other moderate exercises. For not only is the soul restored to serenity, but when a healthy mind is in a healthy body, all becomes healthy and fitted to a better service of God.[41]   *Rome, March, 1548.*

Actually, the essential mortification is to prefer God to the world:

The shortest, and almost the only way to achieve sanctity is to have a horror for all which ·the world loves and embraces.[42]

From the moment of their arrival at the novitiate, Ignatius informed those who offered themselves for the religious life of this. Out of this renunciation of the world spring the mortifications which we have not sought, and they are the best. To them Ignatius opens his heart and ours without restriction.

He wrote from Paris, November 10, 1532, to Isabelle Roser, one of his first penitents at Barcelona:

When I think of your present sickness and suffering, it is impossible that I should not feel [the pain] of it in my soul.

I wish you all well-being and all imaginable prosperity which can help you for the glory and the service of God. Yet I think that sickness and other temporal losses often come from the hand of God our Lord so that we may grow in understanding, and renounce the love of created things; and so that we may reflect especially on the shortness of life, in order that, thinking of eternity, we may adorn our souls. Then, thinking that God visits especially those whom He loves, I can feel neither sadness nor pain. I am persuaded that a servant of God, thanks to illness, becomes a doctor more skilled by half in ordering and directing his life to the glory and to the service of our Lord.

You say how much evil, how many snares and deceits surround you on all sides. I was not surprised at it, and had it been worse, it would not have astonished me. For as soon as you decide and will to labor with all your strength for the glory, honor and service of God our Lord, by that very fact you join battle with the world and raise a standard against it. You dispose yourself to reject great things by embracing lowly things, no longer considering as of any value, greatness or lowliness, honor or dishonor, richness or poverty, love or hatred, welcomes or rebuffs, the fleeting glory of the world, or all the injuries of the times. If our desire is to live in absolute honor and glory in our neighbor's eyes, we will neither be able to be well rooted in God our Lord, nor will it be possible to remain unhurt when affronts are given to us. . . . May the Mother of God help us to be entirely patient and constant because of the thought of those worse injuries and affronts which Christ our Lord has suffered for us, and, on the condition that others commit no sin, may greater injuries come to you so that you can gain more and more merit . . . for they give you the opportunity of gaining the greatest reward which one can gain in this life, and the greatest riches which you can heap up in this world.[43]

Chapter III   AS FRIEND TO FRIEND

St. Ignatius introduces us to the friendship of God by an explanation of meditation and contemplation in which he calls upon the collaboration of all our faculties:

He who gives to another the method and order of a meditation or contemplation ought faithfully to narrate the facts of the contemplation or meditation, going through the points however, only briefly and with a short explanation; because when the person who contemplates, takes the solid foundation of the facts, discussing and reasoning by himself, and meeting with something that makes the facts clearer (whether this happen through his own reasoning, or through the enlightenment of his understanding by divine grace), he thereby enjoys greater spiritual relish and fruit than if he who gives the Exercises had minutely explained and developed the meaning of the facts; for it is not to know much, but it is to understand and savor the matter interiorly, that fills and satisfies the soul.   *Ex. p. 1; 2.*

To enter on the contemplation, at one time kneeling, at another prostrate on the earth, or stretched on the ground with my face upward, now seated, now standing, ever intent on seeking what I desire . . . in the point in which I shall find what I desire, there I will rest without being anxious to proceed to another until I have satisfied myself. *Ex. p. 29; 76.*

If the person considering the Lord's prayer find in one or two words good matter for thought and spiritual relish and consolation he should not be anxious to pass on even though the hour be spent on that one word.   *Ex. p. 80; 254.*

When by reasoning and intelligence Ignatius has strengthened himself by a contemplation of truth, in his fervent love he will let himself be carried away by divine grace.

Thus after a cold consideration of sin, there follows:

An exclamation of wonder with intense affection, running through all creatures in my mind, how they have suffered me to live, and have preserved me in life; how the angels, who are the sword of the divine justice, have borne with me, and have guarded and prayed for me; how the saints have been interceding and praying for me; and the heavens, the sun, the moon, the stars, and the elements, the fruits of the earth, the birds, the fishes, and the animals; and the earth, how it has not opened to swallow me up, creating new hells that I might suffer there forever.   *Ex. p. 25; 60.*

This exercise is repeated three times and ends with:

The first colloquy to our Lady, that she may obtain for me grace from her Son and Lord for three things: the first, that I may feel an interior knowledge of my sins, and a detestation for them; the second, that I may feel the disorder of my actions, in order that, abhorring it, I may amend and order myself aright; the third, to beg for a knowledge of the world in order that, abhorring it, I may put away from myself worldly and vain things. Then one *Hail Mary.*

The second colloquy will be the same to the Son, in order that He may obtain for me these gifts from the Father. Then the *Anima Christi.*

> Soul of Christ, make me holy.
> Body of Christ, be my salvation.
> Blood of Christ, make me forget myself.
> Water from Christ's side, make me clean.

Passion of Christ, make me strong.
Oh, good Jesus hear me.
Hide me within thy wounds.
Do not allow me to be separated from Thee.
Defend me from the evil enemy.
Call me at the hour of my death.
And command that I come to Thee,
So that with Thee I may praise Thee
Forever and ever, Amen.

The third colloquy will be the same to the Father, that the same eternal Lord may grant them to me. Then a *Pater Noster*.

Two meditations, one in the course of the Exercises, "The Kingdom," the other at their climax, "The Contemplation for Obtaining Love," will show by what steps the soul is invited to enter into the mystery:

The call of the temporal king helps to contemplate the life of the eternal King.

The preparatory prayer consists in asking the grace from God our Lord that all my intentions, actions and operations may be ordered solely to the service and praise of His divine Majesty.

The first prelude is a composition of place, seeing the spot. It will be here to see with the eyes of the imagination the synagogues, towns, and villages through which Christ our Lord used to preach.

The second, to ask for the grace which I desire. It is here I will ask the grace from our Lord, that I may not be deaf to His call, but prompt and diligent to accomplish His most holy will.

The first point is to place before my eyes a human king elected by our Lord God Himself, whom all princes and all Christians reverence and obey.

The second is to consider how this king speaks to all his subjects, saying: "My will is to reduce to subjection all the land of the infidels; wherefore whoever desires to come with me must be contented with the food that I eat, with the drink and the clothing that I have, etc. In like manner he

43

must labor as I do during the day, and watch during the night in order that afterwards he may have part with me in the victory, as he has had in the hard work."

The third is to consider what good subjects ought to answer to a king so liberal and so kind; and consequently if any one did not welcome the request of such a king, how would he deserve to be blamed by all the world, and held as a slothful knight.

The second part of this Exercise consists in applying the above example of the temporal king to Christ our Lord, in the three aforesaid points.

And as regards the first point, if we consider the temporal king's summons to his subjects, how much more worthy of consideration is it to see Christ our Lord, the eternal King, and before Him the whole world, all of whom and each in particular He calls, and says: "My will is to conquer the whole world, and all enemies, and thus to enter into the glory of My Father. Whoever therefore desires to come with Me must labor with Me, in order that following Me in pain, he may likewise follow Me in glory."

The second point is to consider that all who have the use of judgment and reason will offer their whole selves for labor.

The third point is that those who wish to show greater affection, and to signalize themselves in every kind of service of their eternal King and universal Lord, not only will offer their whole persons to labor, but also by acting against their own sensuality, and their carnal and worldly love, will make offers of greater worth and moment saying:

"Eternal Lord of all things, I make my oblation with Thy favor and help, in the presence of Thine infinite goodness, and in the sight of Thy glorious mother, and of all the saints of the heavenly court, protesting that I wish and desire, and that it is my deliberate determination (provided only it be to Thy greater service and praise), to imitate Thee in bearing all insults and reproaches, and all poverty, as well actual poverty as poverty of spirit, if only Thy divine Majesty be pleased to choose and receive me to this life and state."

Ex. pp. 33 ff.; 91 ff.

Contemplation for obtaining Love.

Two things are to be noted here: The first is that love ought to be found in deeds rather than words.

The second is, that love consists in mutual interchange on either side, that is to say, in the lover giving and communicating with the beloved what he has or can give, and on the other hand, in the beloved sharing with the lover, so that if the one has knowledge, honor, riches, he share it with him who has them not, and thus the one share all with the other. The usual preparatory prayer.

The first prelude is a composition of place, and it is here to see myself standing before God our Lord and His angels and saints who are interceding for me.

The second prelude is to ask for what I want. It will be here to ask for an interior knowledge of the many and great benefits I have received, that, thoroughly grateful, I may in all things love and serve His divine Majesty.

The first point is to call to mind the benefits I have received, of my creation, redemption, and the particular gifts, dwelling with great affection on how much God our Lord has done for me, and how much He has given me of that which He has; and consequently, how much He desires to give me Himself insofar as He can according to His divine ordinance; and then to reflect in myself what I, on my side, with great reason and justice, ought to offer and give to His divine Majesty, that is to say, all things that are mine, and myself with them, saying, as one who makes an offering with great affection:

"Take, O Lord, and receive all my liberty, my memory, my understanding, and all my will, whatsoever I have and possess. Thou hast given all these things to me; to Thee, O Lord, I restore them: all are Thine, dispose of them all according to Thy will. Give me love of Thee and Thy grace, for this is enough for me."

The second point is to consider how God dwells in creatures, in the elements giving them being, in the plants giving them growth, in animals giving them feeling, and in men

45

giving them understanding, and so in me giving me being, life, feeling, and causing me to understand; making likewise of me a temple, since I am created to the likeness and image of His divine Majesty; and then reflecting on myself in the same way as has been said in the first point, or in any other way that I shall feel to be better. And let the same be done with regard to each of the following points.

The third point is to consider how God works and labors for me in all created things on the face of the earth, that is He behaves as one who labors, as in the heavens, elements, plants, fruit, cattle, giving them being, preserving them, giving them growth and feeling, and then to reflect on myself.

The fourth point is to see how all good things and all gifts descend from above, as my limited power from the supreme and infinite Might on high, and in the same way, justice, goodness, pity, mercy . . . just as the rays descend from the sun, and waters from the spring. Then to conclude by reflecting on myself, as has been said before.

Colloquy and *Pater Noster.*   *Ex. pp. 74 ff.; 230 ff.*

The colloquy is made properly as one friend speaks to another, or a servant to his master; at one time asking for some favor, at another blaming oneself for some evil committed, now informing him of one's affairs and seeking counsel in them.   *Ex. p. 23; 54.*

The following lessons addressed to the scholastics at Coimbra show us how much the thought of Ignatius is rooted in his meditation and nourished by it:

As recompense He [Christ] has given us Himself, giving Himself as a brother in our flesh, as the price of our salvation on the Cross, as the food and companion of our pilgrimage in the Eucharist. Ah, how poor a soldier is he who has not been induced to work for the honor of such a prince by such recompense!

. . . In a certain way He has deprived Himself of the most perfect happiness, of His goods to give them to us, taking upon Himself all our miseries to free us from them, desiring to be sold in order to redeem us, dishonored to

glorify us, poor to enrich us, suffering death in such igno-
minies and torments to give us an immortal life of happiness. . . .

. . . You live in an age when you must show your desires
by your works. Look around you: where is the divine Majesty honored, where is His tremendous greatness venerated,
where is His most holy will obeyed?

. . . See the misery into which souls are plunged. . . .

. . . What need there is to prepare yourselves for all manner of work and struggle to make of yourselves efficient instruments of divine grace for such a work! Especially when
there are so few loyal workers "who do not seek their own
advantage, but that of Jesus Christ" (Phil. 2:21).[44]

Rome, May 7, 1547.

St. Ignatius wished:

That all the members of the Society should accustom themselves to have God before them in all things and that they
should be taught to lift their hearts to Him, not only in their
prayers, but also in all their other occupations, dedicating
and offering them so as to have the same devotion in actions
as in their meditations.[45]

Chapter IV LOVE FOR LOVE

All the meditations on the mysteries of the life of Christ have no other purpose than to put us into personal contact with God, from which contact love will flow:

Above all, think that your Lord loves you, and return to Him love for love.[46]

Venice, September 11, 1536. To Sister Teresa Rejadella.

I remind you, my Lady, that the providence of our most loving Father and most wise physician normally deals thus with those whom He loves much. The more quickly He desires to conduct a soul to participation in eternal happiness after the present life, the more He purifies it by sufferings in this world in which His only wish is that we may remain in peace with our love. But He spurs on His elect not only by desire of heaven, but also by a distaste for this earth. This latter serves to increase our glory if we receive it with the patience and with the gratitude with which we should accept the gifts of His paternal love, from which come lashes as well as caresses.

And if there is in this world a sure means to avoid anguish

of soul, it is to force ourselves to conform our will entirely to
God's good pleasure. For as soon as God has fully captured
our soul, no one can take Him away from us against our will.
Then there are no accidents of this life which should give us
pain, or trouble us much, when we consider that all sorrow
comes only from the loss of something we love, or from the
fear of losing it.[47]

Rome, January 20, 1554. To Maria Frassona del Gesso.

Make no fuss over evil, shameful, or sensual thoughts, nor
over your sorrows or your coldness when they are against
your will. Neither St. Peter nor St. Paul ever secured im-
munity from this trial. We do not completely succeed, but
we gain a great deal when we pay no attention to these
temptations. Just as I shall not achieve my salvation by the
good works of the good angels, so I shall not be harmed by
the evil thoughts and weaknesses which the evil spirits, the
world and the flesh present to me. God our Lord only asks
of me that my soul be entirely submitted to His divine
Majesty. A soul thus submissive makes its body, whether it
will or no, be conformed to the divine will. This is our greatest struggle, and the good pleasure of the eternal and sovereign Bounty.[48]

Venice, September 11, 1536. To Sister Teresa Rejadella.
We have only to confide in:

The eternal love which is more eager to give us sanctity
than we are to desire it.[49]

Rome, May 7, 1547. To the scholastics at Coimbra.
This eternal love stirs up our own, for there is only one
legitimate ambition:

To love God, and, as a reward for this love, nothing else
than to love Him more and more.[50]

A love and desire for all perfection should take the place
of fear of offending, in order to gain the greatest glory for
God, and praise for Christ, our Creator and Lord.

Const. VI, v.

Nevertheless:

Although it is above all things praiseworthy to serve God
greatly out of pure love, yet we ought to praise much the

49

fear of His divine Majesty, because not only is filial fear a pious and most holy thing, but even servile fear, when a man does not rise to anything better and more useful, is of great help to him to escape from mortal sin; and, after he has escaped from it, he easily attains to filial fear, which is altogether acceptable and pleasing to God our Lord, because it is inseparable from divine love. *Ex. p. 125; 37.*

He does not love God with all his heart who loves something for itself and not for God.[51]

Paris, June, 1532. To Don Martin de Oñaz.

If you loved God from the depths of your heart, you would understand that to suffer for Him is such a happiness that all the pleasures of the world cannot counterbalance it. I tell you that there are not so many fetters and so many chains at Salamanca that I would not wish more for the love of God, for whom I bear that chain which in your eyes seems too much for me.[52]

To a lady who told him of her sorrow at seeing him in prison he said:

By that [your sorrow] you show that you desire not to be imprisoned by God's love. Does prison seem to you to be such an evil?[53]

Tribulations, *he said*, which are borne for the cause of Jesus Christ should be counted among God's greatest benefits.[54]

If God gives you much suffering, it is a sign that He wants to make you a great saint; and if you want God to make you a great saint, pray Him to give you much to suffer. There is no wood which makes a greater fire of love of God than the wood of the cross which has served Christ to make a sacrifice of infinite love. All the honey which we can gather from the flowers and pleasures of the world has not as much sweetness as the vinegar and gall of Christ, that is to say, the bitterness of the sufferings which we undergo in the company of Christ for love.[55]

To those who will strongly, nothing is difficult, above all in those things which we undertake for the love of our Lord, Jesus Christ.[56]   *Paris, June, 1532. To Don Martin de Oñaz.*

As much as you can, have God always in your heart, and your heart always in God. Love nothing but Him. Think of no other thing but Him. Never take your eyes away from His presence. May His holy will be like the center of all the impulses of your action.[57]

May the life of Christ be the model and, so to speak, the seal of yours. Make yourself stamp the image of His life on you as vividly as you can.[58]

Since the object of your love is God, it has an infinite object. So your finite heart can always advance farther and farther in love.[59]

This is more true since:

To rise to his Creator and embrace at once His love, the man who realizes what God is has no need of the sight of the heavens and the stars; a blade of grass and the tiniest thing that his eye sees is enough for him.[60]

Chapter V THE DISPUTE OF THE ANGELS

If the Exercises *require the use of man's faculties and effort, St. Ignatius knows that the work of God is infinitely more important, but that it is attacked by the work of the demons.*

He has experienced the torments and the struggles of that opposition. It is at that point of combat that the spiritual counselor will intervene to aid the soul in discerning the light of God:

If he who gives the *Exercises* sees that the retreatant is in desolation or temptation, let him not show himself harsh or severe toward him, but kind and encouraging. Let him give the retreatant courage and energy for the future, explaining to him the tricks of the enemy of human nature. Especially let him help him to prepare himself and dispose himself for future consolation.   *Ex. p. 3; 7.*

It belongs to God and His angels to give in their motions true joy and spiritual gladness, removing all sadness and disturbance of mind occasioned by the enemy; while it belongs to him to fight against such joy and spiritual consolation, bringing forward pretended reasons, sophistries, and perpetual fallacies.

It belongs to our Lord alone to grant consolation to the soul without any preceding cause for it, because it belongs to the Creator alone to go in and out of the soul to excite motions in it attracting it entirely to the love of His divine Majesty. *Ex. pp. 111–112; 329–330.*

These are some principles for discerning:

I call it consolation when there is excited in the soul some interior motion by which it begins to be inflamed with the love of its Creator and Lord, and when, consequently, it can love no created thing on the face of the earth in itself, but only in the Creator of them all. Likewise, when the soul sheds tears, moving it to the love of its Lord, whether it be from grief for its sins, or from the Passion of Christ our Lord, or from other things directly ordained to His service and praise. Finally I call consolation every increase of hope, faith and charity, and all interior joy which calls and attracts man to heavenly things, and to the salvation of his own soul, rendering it quiet and tranquil in its Creator and Lord.

Ex. p. 107; 316.

I call desolation darkness and disquiet of soul, an attraction toward low and earthly objects, the disquiet of various agitations and temptations, which move it to diffidence, without hope and without love, when the soul finds itself slothful, tepid, sad, and, as it were, separated from its Creator and Lord. *Ex. p. 107; 317.*

In time of desolation we must never make a change, but remain firm and constant in the state we are in.

Ex. p. 108; 318.

Although in desolation we ought not to change our former resolutions, it is very profitable to make changes vehemently in ourselves in ways that oppose the desolation.

Ex. p. 108; 319.

For as in consolation it is the good spirit that guides and directs us, so in desolation it is the bad spirit, by whose counsels we cannot find the way to any right decision.

Ex. p. 108; 318.

53

When there is consolation without any preceding cause, though there be no deceit in it, inasmuch as it proceeds only from God our Lord . . . distinguish the exact period of the actual consolation from the period which follows it, in which the soul continues fervent and feels the remains of the divine favor and consolation lately received; for in this second period it often happens that by its own thoughts . . . whether by the suggestion of the good or evil spirit, it makes various resolves and plans which are not inspired immediately by God our Lord; and hence it is necessary that they be thoroughly well examined before they receive entire credit and are carried into effect. *Ex. pp. 113–114; 336.*

In the case of those who are making progress from good to better, the good angel touches the soul, gently, lightly and sweetly, as a drop of water entering into a sponge; and the evil spirit touches it sharply and with noise and disturbance, like a drop of water falling on a rock. In the case of those who go from bad to worse, spirits touch it in the contrary manner; and the reason of this difference is the disposition of the soul, according as it is contrary or similar to these angels; for when it is contrary to them, they enter with perceptible commotion and disturbance; but when it is similar to them, they enter in silence, as into their own house, through the open doors. *Ex. p. 113; 335.*

Our enemy has no means more sure, as St. Bernard notes, to make true charity flee the heart than to make the heart advance in that love imprudently, without the control of spiritual wisdom. "Nothing to excess," the philosopher told us. We should follow this principle even in the matter of justice, since we read in Ecclesiastes (7:17) "Do not be excessively just." When we do not preserve that moderation, good is changed into evil and virtue into vice, and from this follow many trials which are contrary to the intention of the one who acts thus.

The first is that he cannot long serve God. So a horse cannot finish its journey when it has worn itself out on the first stages, and then others have to take charge and care for it.

The second is that we can scarcely retain what we have so

hastily acquired. For, as Scripture says (Prov. 13:11), "A fortune got in haste shall be diminished." It is not only diminished, but it collapses completely. "He who runs, strikes his feet." And the higher one is, the more danger if he slips, of falling to the foot of the ladder.

The third is that we run the danger of overloading our boat. For if it is dangerous to have it empty, since it will be battered by temptations, so, if it is overloaded, it will founder.

The fourth is that instead of crucifying the old man, we crucify the new, for in infirmity we cannot practice virtue. According to St. Bernard, this excess brings with it four injustices: we steal strength from the body, fervor from the soul, edification from the neighbor, and honor from God (*De vita solitaria*, i., 1). From this he concludes that he who thus mistreats the living temple of God is guilty of sacrilege. He disedifies the neighbor for the fall of one becomes a scandal to others.[61]

Rome, May 7, 1547. To the scholastics at Coimbra.

So we ought to pay close attention; and if the devil makes us proud, we must humiliate ourselves by considering our sins and miseries; if he discourages us and casts us down, we must raise ourselves up in true faith and hope in the Lord, by recalling to ourselves the good things we have received from Him, and the great love and will with which He desires our salvation; whereas the enemy cares not whether he says true or false, but only whether he conquers us.

If the devil represents justice to me, I in reply speak of mercy. If he represents mercy, I on the contrary speak of justice. Thus should we walk in such a way that we avoid trouble, that the one who mocks us should, in the end, be mocked. Let us confide in this word of Scripture: "Do not be so humble that your humility drives you to folly."[62]

June 18, 1536. To Sister Teresa Rejadella.

It is proper to God to give understanding and not take it away from us; for Him to send hope, and not despair.[63]

Venice, February 12, 1526. To James Cazador.

The characteristic of the divine Bounty is to defend with

55

more power what the devil attacks more fiercely, and to strengthen more solidly what the devil strains to destroy. The difficulty of a work undertaken with repugnance will be matched by the intensity of the joy that follows.[64]

Not only does God reserve an eternal crown in reward for victories over Satan, but even in this life He renders us the mercy of making us stronger in those virtues against which we have already been most violently tempted; and He rewards by an abundance of consolations and delights of spirit the pain and bitterness which our resistance has caused us.[65]

God is always accustomed to give more comfort and consolation in those things in which the devil has struggled to ruin the soul and has not succeeded.[66]

Chapter VI COME AND FOLLOW ME

The grace of graces for Ignatius was to know the will of God in our regard. Starting in June, 1532, he began the custom of closing his letters with this formula which became habitual with him:

I pray and beg God, by His infinite and sovereign goodness, that He give us the grace of knowing His most holy will and of accomplishing it completely.

Paris, to Don Martin de Oñaz.

The only purpose of the Exercises *is to lead us in this search. They note first the principle of it:*

Let all endeavor to have a right intention, not only in their state of life, but also in all particulars, seeking in them always sincerely to serve and please the divine Goodness for itself, and for the charity and singular benefits wherewith it has prevented us, rather than for fear of punishment or hope of reward, though they ought also to draw profit from these; and in all things let them seek God, casting off as much as is possible all love of creatures, that they may place their whole affection on the Creator of them, loving Him in all creatures and them all in Him, according to His most holy and divine Will.   *Summary, 17.*

In every good election, as far as regards ourselves, the eye of our intention ought to be single, looking only to the end for which I was created, which is, for the praise of God our Lord, and for the salvation of my soul. And thus whatever I choose ought to be for this, that it should help me to the end for which I was created; not ordering and drawing the end to the means, but the means to the end. As, for example, it happens that many choose first to marry, which is a means, and secondarily to serve our Lord God in the married state, which service of God is the end. . . . So these do not go straight to God, but wish God to come straight to their inordinate affections.

Nothing then ought to move me to take these or other means, or to deprive myself of them, except only the service and praise of God our Lord, and the eternal salvation of my soul.   *Ex. p. 54; 169.*

Knowing that the designs of God are different for each soul, he thinks that:

There is no error more pernicious among masters of the spiritual life than desiring to govern others by themselves, and thinking that what is good for them is good for all. . . . This is very dangerous. This is to ignore the multiform diversity of the gifts of grace and the variety of the gifts of the Holy Spirit, and not to understand how often graces are different in the same spirit.[68]

The more our soul finds itself alone and in solitude, the fitter it renders itself to approach and unite itself to its Creator and Lord; and the nearer it thus unites itself to Him, the more it disposes itself to receive graces and favors from His divine and supreme Goodness.   *Ex. p. 10; 20.*

Let the soul then give itself freely to divine inspirations:

When the soul is seeking the divine will, it is better and more fitting that its Creator and Lord Himself communicate with the devout soul, inflaming it to love and praise Him, and disposing it for that way of life by which it will best serve Him for the future; so that he who gives the *Exercises* must not himself be influenced or inclined to one side or another, but, keeping as it were in equilibrium like a balance, allow the Creator to act immediately with the creature, and the creature with its Creator and Lord.   *Ex. p. 6; 15.*

In order that the Creator and Lord may more surely work in His creature, if perchance such a soul is affected and inclined inordinately to anything, it will be very profitable for it to strive and to employ all its forces to arrive at the contrary of that to which it is wrongly affected . . . in such a way that the cause for desiring or having one thing or another be solely the service, honor and glory of His divine Majesty.   *Ex. p. 7; 16.*

The love which urges and causes me to choose such or such a thing should descend from on high from the love of God; so that he who chooses feel first in himself that the love which he has more or less for the thing he chooses is solely for the sake of his Creator and Lord.   *Ex. p. 59; 184.*

When we are not indifferent to poverty or riches, it will help much to ask that our Lord should choose us to serve Him in actual poverty, protesting that we desire, petition and ask for it, provided it be to the service and praise of His divine Goodness.   *Ex. p. 49; 157.*

St. Ignatius proposes to us several methods of making a reasonable and good election. This is the first:

The first point is to propose to myself the matter about which I wish to make an election, that is, anything which falls under a mutable election.

Secondly, it is necessary to keep as my aim the end for which I was created, which is to praise God our Lord, and to save my soul; and at the same time to find myself indifferent, without any inordinate affection; so that I be not more inclined or disposed to take than to leave the thing proposed, nor more disposed to leave it than to take it, but I must be, as it were, in equilibrium on a balance, ready to follow that which I shall feel to be more for the glory and praise of God our Lord and for the salvation of my soul.

The third point is to beg God our Lord that He may be pleased to move my will, and place in my soul that which I

59

ought to do in regard to the matter proposed, which may be more to His praise and glory; turning over the matter well in my mind, and making a choice in conformity with His most holy will and good pleasure.

The fourth is to consider, reasoning as to what advantages and profit will accrue to me, or what inconveniences and dangers if I hold the proposed matter solely for the praise of our Lord God and for the salvation of my soul.

The fifth point is, after I have thus turned over and reasoned on everything with regard to the matter proposed to see to what side reason most inclines; and to follow the weightier motions of reason, and not any sensual ones.

The sixth point is that, after having made such an election, he who has made it must with great diligence betake himself to prayer, in the presence of God our Lord, and offer Him that election, that His divine Majesty may be pleased to receive and confirm it, if it be to His greater service and praise.   *Ex. pp. 57–58; 179–183.*

PART II: THE SOCIETY OF JESUS

During twenty years of prayer, Ignatius continued his search for the will of God. Gradually it became evident to him that God wished him to dedicate himself to fight with Jesus Christ, his Master, for the conquest of His kingdom. Therefore he gathered together companions in arms and placed them at the disposal of the pope to be sent on missions throughout the world.

Thus he instituted a new religious order, THE SOCIETY OF JESUS.

Chapter 1 TO FIGHT UNDER THE
STANDARD OF THE CROSS

In 1546, when Ignatius refused the bishopric which Emperor Ferdinand had asked for Fr. Claude LeJay, he said in his petition to the pope:

The other religious orders of the Church's army are like frontline troops drawn up in massive battalions. We are like light-armed soldiers ready for sudden battles, going from one side to the other, now here, now there. And for this we must be unencumbered and free from all responsibility of this type.[69]

For this new kind of military service, new regulations were required:

Although it be the sovereign wisdom and goodness of God our Creator and Lord, which is to preserve, govern and advance in His holy service this least Society of Jesus, as it has vouchsafed to begin the same, and on your part the interior law of charity and love, which the Holy Spirit is accustomed to write and imprint in the hearts of men, is to help thereunto rather than any exterior constitutions; yet, because the sweet disposition of divine providence requires the cooperation of His creatures, and the Vicar of Christ our Lord, has so appointed, and the examples of saints and reason itself teach us so in our Lord, we think it necessary that constitutions should be written, which may help us according to the spirit of our institute, to greater progress in the way of God's service upon which we have entered.

Preface to the Constitutions.

These are the essential outlines of those Constitutions:

Since the Society, which was not instituted by human means, can neither be preserved nor strengthened by them, but by the grace of almighty God and our Lord Jesus Christ, we must have confidence in Him that He will preserve and promote that work which He has deigned to begin for His service and glory and for the aid of souls. And in accord with this hope, the first and most fitting means to achieve it will be that of prayer and the holy Sacrifice of the Mass.

Among the means which can preserve and increase not only the body but also the spirit of the Society and make it achieve the end which it proposes to itself, those means which unite the instrument to God and which dispose it to be completely governed by the hand of its Lord are more efficacious than those which dispose it with regard to men. Such are integrity, virtue, and above all charity and a pure intention in serving God, intimate union with Him in spiritual exercises, and a sincere zeal for procuring the salvation of souls for the glory of Him who created and redeemed them, without seeking any other advantage.

Let all who belong to the Society apply themselves to the pursuit of solid and perfect virtues and of spiritual things; and account these of greater moment than learning or other natural or human gifts; for they are the interior things from which force must flow to the exterior for the end proposed to us.

Once this foundation has been laid, those natural means which fit the instrument of God and our Lord for helping the neighbor will also aid in the conservation and growth of this entire body, provided however that they are acquired and used sincerely for the service of God alone, not that our

64

confidence may depend on them, but rather that by them we may cooperate with the divine grace in accord with the order of His divine providence. For He wishes that both the natural gifts which He gives us as Creator, and the supernatural gifts which He gives as the Author of grace be referred to His glory. So we should diligently seek human gifts, or those which are acquired through our labor, and especially accurate and solid doctrine, and a manner of proposing them to the people in sermons and lectures, and a manner of dealing with people and influencing them.

Const. X, 1, 2; 3.

It is a man's humility which will win him God's assistance:

We care little whether niceties and beauties of human rhetoric adorn our discourses. After a great many experiences we think that our Lord in His infinite and sovereign bounty does not forget us and, despite our littleness, and without any merit, that He aids and helps many souls by our instrumentality.[70]

Rome, December 19, 1538. To Isabelle Roser.

This readiness to answer God's call must be safeguarded at all costs. Jesuits will be simple soldiers. St. Ignatius wrote to Ferdinand I, king of the Romans, who wished to make Fr. LeJay a bishop:

May the divine Majesty put and imprint in your soul how much more you can help us to go forward according to our least profession, in this way particularly, by demanding our service without giving us any honor whatsoever. For if I should wish to imagine or to conjecture some means to destroy or to demolish this Society, this means, of accepting bishoprics, would be one of the greatest, if not the greatest of all.[71]   *Rome, December 8, 1546.*

The society must ambition no other honor than to resemble Jesus Christ:

They must diligently observe, esteeming it of great importance and of the highest moment in the sight of our Creator and Lord, how much it helps and contributes to progress in spiritual life, to abhor wholly and not in part what the world loves and embraces, and to accept and desire with their whole strength whatsoever Christ our Lord loved and embraced. For, as worldly men, who follow the things of the world, love and with great diligence seek honors, reputation and the credit of a great name upon earth, as the world teaches them, so those who are advancing in spirit and seriously follow Christ our Lord, love and earnestly desire things which are altogether the contrary; that is, to be clothed with the same garment and with the livery of their Lord for His love and reverence; insomuch that if it could be without offense of the divine Majesty and without sin on the part of their neighbor, they would wish to suffer reproaches, slanders and injuries, and to be treated and accounted as fools (without at the same time giving any occasion for it) because they desire to imitate and resemble in some sort their Creator and Lord Jesus Christ, and to be clothed with His garments and livery; since he clothed Himself with the same for our greater spiritual good, and gave us an example, that in all things, as far as by the assistance of God's grace we can, we may seek to imitate and follow Him, seeing He is the true way that leads men to life.[72]

Ignatius stirs up the ardor of the young men who have offered themselves to fight with him for the kingdom of Jesus Christ in the following words:

For the love of Jesus Christ, forgetting the past, in imitation of St. Paul's example, keep your gaze fixed on the great distance which remains to be traveled on the road of virtue. Consider as avowed enemies of your soul negligence, lack of generosity, and laziness, which cool and weaken the desire of advancing in the spiritual life and in learning. Place before your eyes as models for your imitation, not the cowardly and the weak, but the brave and the fervent. Blush to be surpassed by the children of the world, who are more solicitous to acquire the goods of time than you are to gain the goods of eternity. Be confounded to see that they run more swiftly to death than you to life. Think yourselves capable of very little, if a courtier, to gain the favor of an earthly prince, serves him with more fidelity than you serve the king of heaven; and if a soldier, for a shadow of glory and for the wretched share of the spoils which he expects from a battle won, fights against his enemies and struggles with more valor than you do to conquer the world, the devil and yourselves, and to win by that victory the kingdom of heaven and an immortal glory.

The bow is broken if it be stretched too tight, but the soul is lost if it is relaxed. . . . Take care, then, to revivify and keep alive in yourselves a holy fervor so that you can give yourselves entirely to the study of perfection and of learning. Regard it as certain that in the one as in the other, one act animated by that fervor will advance you farther than a thousand acts done with laxness. Believe also that what a negligent man gains only with great work in many years, the fervent man obtains easily and in a short time. By not being willing to struggle against themselves, the slothful never arrive, or arrive only very late, at true peace of soul, and the possession of some virtue. On the other hand, the fervent and the courageous arrive at both of them in a short time. As far as joy is concerned, however little of it we have in this life, not the slothful, but the fervent in God's service are those who enjoy it. For it is to the conqueror that the hidden manna will be given.[73]

Rome, June 7, 1547. To the scholastics at Coimbra. Toward the end of his life, the doctor had forbidden St. Ignatius to think of "things which could make him sad, for that would aggravate his illness:"

I asked myself what things could make me sad, and I found none, unless that the pope would completely destroy the Society. But even on that, I think that if I recollected myself in prayer for a quarter of an hour, I would be as happy, and even happier, than before.[74]

Chapter II   POOR WITH CHRIST POOR

In the Exercises *St. Ignatius proposes poverty as the first trait of likeness to Jesus Christ:*

Supposing equal praise and glory to the divine Majesty, the better to imitate Christ our Lord, and to become actually more like to Him, I desire and choose rather poverty with Christ poor, than riches; contempt with Christ contemned than honors; and I desire to be esteemed as useless and foolish for Christ's sake, who was first held to be such, rather than to be accounted wise and prudent in this world.

Ex. p. 43; 167.

Ignatius will make poverty the safeguard of the Society:

Poverty, as a firm wall of religion, should be loved and maintained in its purity so far as it can be by the help of God's grace. *Summary 23.*

It is poverty which will assure independence with regard to men, and detachment in the service of God:

Let the trust of the Society be placed in God alone whom, by His favor, we serve. Without any revenues He will pro-

vide for us all things which will help to His greater praise
and service. *Const. VI, ii, 2.*

When the Holy Father or a superior shall send the professed or coadjutors to labor in the vineyard of the Lord,
they may not ask viaticum for the journey; but let them
generously offer themselves to be sent insofar as it seems to
them that it will be for the greater glory of God. That is, on
foot or on horseback, with money or without it. And they
must by all means be prepared to do that which he who
sends them thinks more fitting and for the greater edification
of all. *Const. VI, ii, 13. i.*

They must be ready to beg from door to door whenever
obedience or necessity shall require it. *Const. VI, ii, 10.*

*Poverty is something joyfully chosen out of love. Indeed
for a religious:*

The fear of poverty frightens him more than poverty itself.[75]

Let all love poverty as a mother. *Const. III, i, 25.*

In order that poverty, and that peace which it brings with
it, may be preserved in its purity. . . . *Const. VI, ii, 12.*

In those things which deal with the matter of food, sleep
and the rest of the necessities and conveniences of life, let
any privation come out of devotion, not out of obligation.
Const. VI, ii, 16.

If we give freely what we have freely received, the Lord
alone will be our reward according to our Institute, and He
will be our great gain. *Const. IV, xv, 4.*

*This deliverance and this detachment are so much the
fruit of poverty that the Christian, even if he remain in the
world, will find in it his liberty:*

He who is not called to that first and sublime degree of
perfection which consists in possessing nothing but God,
should mount at least to the second, that is, let it be he who
possesses his possessions, not they which possess him. If he
does not leave them for God, let him order them to God.
And, no matter how great they are, let him consider them of
less worth than that one thing which the Gospel says is
necessary.[76]

It is in the following way that Ignatius traces the way of poverty for his brothers or his friends who remained in the world:

The fact that in this life a man accepts sleeplessness, anxiety and cares to build and increase a stately home, yearly income and a standard of living, in order to leave a great name and a great memory on earth, it is not for me to condemn. But I cannot praise him, since, according to St. Paul, "We should use things as not using them, possess them as not possessing them, have a wife as not having one, for the face of the world is very fleeting." If you have ever thought so, or if you think so now, I beg you by the love of God our Lord to use all your strength to acquire honor in heaven, memory and renown before the Lord who will judge us. Since He has given you earthly goods in abundance, use them to acquire eternal goods.[77]

Paris, June, 1532. To Don Martin de Oñaz.

That one should abandon his goods in such a way as to:

Leave to others the means to feed horses, dogs and game, to maintain rank, luxury and ostentation, I cannot consent to this. St. Gregory mentions among other degrees of perfection, "to leave all that one possesses to relations and parents, and to follow Christ our Lord." But he judges it better to leave all by distributing it among the poor according to the word, "if you wish to be perfect. . . ." I think then that it is better to give to the poor when they are in greater need than our relatives; but in equal need, we should rather give to our relatives than to others.[78]

Venice, February 12, 1536. To James Cazador.

Do much good to the poor, *he writes to his brother*, to orphans and to those in need. He should not be avaricious to whom God our Lord has been so generous.[79]

Paris, June, 1532. To Don Martin de Oñaz.

ॐ

Chapter III THE LIVERY OF CHRIST

He is not great among you who was formerly great in the world, but he who makes himself small for Christ.[80]

In proportion to the height of a building, so must be the depth of the foundation.[81]

For that purpose:

It will help very much to apply ourselves with all possible devotion to those offices wherein humility and charity are chiefly practiced; and generally speaking, the closer one shall bind himself to God, and the more liberal he shall show himself in His sovereign Majesty, by so much he shall find God more liberal toward him, and be daily more fit to receive in greater abundance His graces and spiritual gifts. *Summary 19.*

They [superiors] should take special care in mortifying noblemen and scholars because, if these men do good, they will do great service to God, but if they do evil, they will do much harm.[82]

If our faults humiliate us, we must not let them deprive us of courage:

If any fall publicly into some fault which seems to cause

71

them discredit and dishonor, let them not be cast down, nor lose courage or hope. But let them give thanks to God who, by permitting that fall, has made them realize the weakness of their virtue, so that they might not be more esteemed for that which in reality they were not.[83]

Humility, by making us sincere, establishes us in liberty and love:

There is no one in the house by whom I am not edified, except myself.[84]

One of the most frequent prayers of St. Ignatius was:

Give me, Lord, a loving humility and also a loving reverence and respect.[85]

This genuine humility is the best source of joy. To a young novice, Francis Coster, who had the reputation of laughing more than the others:

Francis, I hear that you are always laughing. Yes, my son, I want you to laugh and be happy in the Lord. A religious has no reason to be in desolation, but he has many reasons to rejoice. In order to be ever joyous and gay, be ever humble and ever obedient.[86]

On the thirtieth of January, 1551, Ignatius tried to resign the generalship of the Society of Jesus by the following letter:

Considering realistically and without passion my manifold imperfections, sins, and weaknesses, I have often thought that I do not have the qualities necessary to have charge of the Society, which I now have because the Society has desired it and has imposed it on me. In the name of the Father and of the Son and of the Holy Spirit, my only God and Creator, I resign and renounce simply and absolutely that government, asking and begging in our Lord with all my soul that the professed and all those whom they wish to assemble for that purpose be willing to accept my oblation, so well justified, so that His holy will may be done in all, for His greater glory and for the greatest advantage of all souls and of the entire Society, ever considering all in view of His divine and greater praise and glory.[87]

Chapter IV LIKE THE ANGELS . . .

What concerns the vow of chastity needs no explanation, as it is plain how perfectly it ought to be observed; that is, by endeavoring to imitate angelical purity in cleanness of both body and mind. *Summary 28.*

Chapter V AT THE VOICE OF JESUS CHRIST

Since he has placed his Society by a special vow at the service of the pope, St. Ignatius demands before all else an immediate and absolute obedience to the Church:

Laying aside all private judgment, we ought to keep our minds prepared and ready to obey in all things the true Spouse of Christ our Lord, which is our holy Mother, the hierarchical Church. *Ex. p. 121; 353.*

This rule is more necessary for those whom a zealous spiritual life could lead astray:

You must take great care lest those who spend their time in prolonged prayers, and pass long hours in meditation on divine things become brusque and hardened, obstinate in their own views, and lest, by their fault, that which is the medicine of all spiritual ills become poison.

There are some, moreover, who believe that everything which they experience in prayer comes from God, and who regard their feelings as those of God, from which they may not deviate. Often they deceive themselves.

We must not submit that which is certain to our own feelings, no matter how pious and divine they may appear; on the contrary, we should bend our feelings and our thoughts, doubtful and deceptive as they are, to the most sure and most certain rule of faith and of holy men. For truly it is not right to sacrifice certain things to things which are doubtful; but it is right to enlighten and strengthen doubtful things by those which are certain.[88]

St. Ignatius makes obedience the distinguishing virtue of his Society:

More easily may we suffer ourselves to be surpassed by other religious orders in fasting, watching and other severities in diet and apparel, which according to their institute and rule every one does piously practice; but in true and perfect obedience and the abnegation of our will and judgment, I greatly desire, most dear brethren, that those who serve God in this Society should be conspicuous, and that the true and genuine progeny of the same should, as it were, be distinguished by this mark.[89]   *Rome, March 26, 1553.*

To the religious of the Society in Portugal.

There are three ways to obey; the first consists in obeying when I am commanded in the name of holy obedience, and this degree is good; the second consists in obeying when I receive only a simple command, and this degree is better; the third consists in anticipating the command, and carrying out that which I see is the superior's inclination even though he gives me no order, and this third degree is much more perfect than the other two.[90]

Let us then take care to direct all our forces toward that virtue of obedience, which we ought to render first to the sovereign pontiff, and then to the superiors of the Society; in such a way that all things to which obedience can in charity be extended, we be as prompt as possible to their voice, as if it came from Christ our Lord, since we obey Him out of love of Him and respect for Him.   *Const. VI, i, 1.*

For the superior is not to be obeyed because he is prudent or virtuous, or excells in any other divine gift whatsoever it be; but only for this, that he is in the place of God, and has authority from Him who says, "He that heareth you, heareth me, and he that despiseth you, despiseth me."

Wherefore I desire that you should earnestly endeavor, with all care and diligence, to acknowledge Christ in every

75

superior, and with great devotion reverence and obey in him the divine Majesty.

. . . that they regard, not the individual whom they obey, but in him Christ our Lord, for whose love they obey.

Moreover, I desire that this should be thoroughly understood and deeply imprinted in your minds that this first degree of obedience is very base, and that it is not worthy of the name of virtue unless it pass to the second degree, making the will of the superior our will, and so agreeing with the same, that not only is there external fulfillment of the command, but also agreement of will; that so both may be of the one mind in willing and not willing the same.

And so, you must always be very careful that you never seek to wrest the superior's will (which you ought to hold for the will of God Himself) unto your own; for that would be, not to conform your will unto God's, but to endeavor to rule His will by yours, inverting the order of His divine Wisdom.[91]   *Rome, March 26, 1553.*

To the religious of the Society in Portugal.

Prudence is not the virtue of him who obeys, but of him who commands, and the only way of acting prudently in obedience is to renounce prudence, rather than renounce obedience.[92]

"Lean not upon thy own prudence," says the Holy Scripture (Prov. 3:5). And even in worldly matters those who are wise judge it to be the part of a prudent man not to trust his own wisdom, especially in his own cause, in which, when the mind is troubled, one can hardly be a good judge.

And if in matters concerning ourselves we are to prefer the judgment and counsel of another, who is not our own superior, how much more should we prefer the counsel and judgment of the superior to whom we have yielded ourselves to be directed, as to one who is in place of God, and interpreter of His divine will.

Would that this obedience of the understanding and judgment were as much understood and put into practice by men, as it is pleasing to God, and necessary for all those who live in religion! For as in the celestial bodies, so that one sphere might receive motion and influence from another, it is necessary that the inferior globe be subject — in the manner appropriate to physical bodies — to the superior; so among men, so that one might be moved by another's authority, it is necessary that he who depends upon another be subject and subordinate, to the end that he may receive some virtue and influence from him who commands. Now this kind of subjection and obedience can in no wise exist, unless the will and judgment of the inferior agree with the will and judgment of the superior.[93]

To the religious of the Society in Portugal.

He often said:

He who does not have obedience of the understanding, but only of the will has only one foot in the religious life.[94]

We must take care to act in a spirit of love and not under the unsettling influence of fear, so that we obey with great promptness, spiritual joy and perseverance. So it is necessary that all show to their superiors a great respect; that they trust them, and reverence Jesus Christ in them; that they love them with all their heart as fathers in Him; and that they act through a spirit of love in all things. Let them hide nothing from them either of external or internal affairs, but rather wish that superiors know absolutely all their affairs so that they can direct them better in the way of salvation and perfection. *Const. VI, i.*

There perishes that renowned simplicity of blind obedience, when we call in question the justice of the command, and perhaps we even condemn the superior because he bids us do such things as are not very pleasing to us; there fails humility, for although on the one hand we obey, yet on the other we prefer ourselves before our superior; there fails fortitude in difficult enterprises, and (to conclude in brief) the whole force and dignity of this virtue is lost. And in their place there arise pain, trouble, reluctance, weariness, murmurings, excuses and other vices of no small importance by which the value and merit of obedience is wholly destroyed.

And because you are interiorly conscious that you have

77

submitted to this yoke of obedience for the love of God, to the end that you might, in following the superior's will, more surely follow the divine will, do not doubt that the most faithful charity of our Lord continually directs you and leads you the right way by the hands of those whom He has made your superiors. Wherefore hear their voice just as if it were the voice of Christ.

The last means, both easier and more secure, to subject your understanding is to decide interiorly that whatever the superior commands is the commandment and will of almighty God Himself; and just as you instantly bend all the forces of your mind to believe the propositions of the Catholic faith, so, in carrying out the commands of your superiors, you must be borne alone by a kind of blind impulse, anxious to obey.

And if anything occurs to you different from the superior's opinion, and even after you have humbly commended the matter to God it seems that you should mention it, there is nothing to hinder you from proposing it to him. But in such matters, lest self-love and your own judgment deceive you, you should be careful to remain both before and after manifesting it most indifferent, not only as to the taking up or relinquishing the matter in question, but also approving and thinking the superior's opinion better, whatever it be.

And what I have said of obedience is to be equally observed by every private person toward his immediate superiors, and by the rectors and local superiors toward the provincials, by the provincials toward the general, and the general toward the superior whom God has placed over him, His Vicar on earth. The purpose of this is that thus a perfect distinction of degrees, and consequently peace and charity may be preserved. For without this, right government cannot be maintained, either in our Society or in any other congregation.

Divine Providence uses this procedure in arranging all things smoothly, and bringing them to their appointed ends, the lowest being governed by intermediate, and these latter by the highest.

From this principle springs also that subordination in angels of one hierarchy to another, and that perfect harmony of all things which are moved, each one in its determined place and sphere. Their revolutions and motions proceed in an orderly and gradual way from one supreme Mover down to the lowest.

We see the same thing upon earth, both in all well-ordered states and, especially, in the ecclesiastical hierarchy, whose members and functions are all derived from one universal Vicar of Christ on earth. And in proportion as this disposition and order is more exactly kept, the whole government is better. On the other hand, everyone has seen what grievous damages have befallen various congregations by neglecting this.[95]   *To the religious of the Society in Portugal.*

Strive then:

To advance in the spirit that whatever the superior commands is the commandment and will of God Himself, so much so that as you determine without hesitation and with full submission to embrace the truths which the Catholic faith proposes to you, so you proceed, with all the impetuosity of a will whose only tendency is to obey, without examining anything, without seeing anything, to do all that the superior commands you.[96]

To the religious of the Society in Portugal.

In a word:

I ought no longer to be my own, but my Creator's, and his who holds the Creator's place to govern me. And by his hands I should let myself be led, as if I were a piece of wax, no matter what he wishes to do with me, when there is question of writing or receiving a letter, of talking or not talking, and to this or that person. And I must use all my devotion and readiness in carrying out all that I shall be commanded, persuading myself that all that is commanded has been commanded for my own good.[97]

. . . leaving unfinished anything whatsoever, even a letter of the alphabet begun and not ended. Let us, in the Lord, direct all our powers and our intention to this point, that among us holy obedience be perfect in every detail both in execution and in will and judgment, performing with great speed, spiritual joy and perseverance whatever shall be commanded us, persuading ourselves that all things are just, denying — with a certain kind of blind obedience — any contrary opinion or judgment of our own, doing this in every command of the superior, provided we cannot certainly discern any sin in it. Let everyone persuade himself that those who live under obedience must allow themselves to be carried and ruled by divine Providence in their superiors as if they were a dead body, which permits itself to be carried anywhere and treated in any manner, or like an old man's staff which serves the one who holds it in his hand wherever and for whatever use he pleases. For he who obeys in this way ought to do everything in which his superior wishes to employ him with gaiety of heart, being persuaded that in this way he will correspond better with the divine will than by anything else which he could do by following his own will and a contrary opinion.

Summary 34–36.

The more the inferiors depend on their superiors, the more love, obedience and union there will be between them.

Const. VIII, i, 26.

Let those who hold the first places in the Society be outstanding by reason of their good example, being completely united with their superior; and let them always obey him promptly and humbly.   *Const. VIII, i, 3.*

A little before his death, St. Ignatius dictated to Fr. Giovanni Filippo Vitti some last instructions concerning obedience:

I should not make any distinction between superior and superior, considering whether it is the major superior, a mediate superior, or the lowest superior who commands me. But in all of them I should recognize God whose place they hold. Otherwise, if we take account of persons, all the force of obedience is lost.[98]

To the scholastics of the college of Gandia in Spain, St. Ignatius showed the merit and the effects of a perfect obedience:

But apart from examples, reason teaches us the same lesson. We all hold that manner of life best which renders the most pleasing service to God. If so, we must surely hold, too, that of all sacrifices none is more acceptable than obedience. "For obedience is better than sacrifices, and to hearken rather than to offer the fat of rams" (1 Kings 15:22). For there can be no greater sacrifice than the offering up of our will, judgment and liberty, which make up the most noble part of man. This manner of life, too, has another source of singular merit, inasmuch as it bears a likeness to that of a continual martyrdom in those who have the right spirit. . . . For our self-will is, as it were, beheaded, and exchanged for the will of Christ our Lord, made known to us through His vice-gerent. Nor does it, as in the case of the martyr, cut short only the desire of life, but all our desires at once.

Besides, in casting his burden upon the superior, he removes the heavy load of his own self-will and personal anxieties and is thereby freed from a thousand doubts and perplexities. Then, having abandoned all to the superior, the religious must not usurp the right of governing himself. Let him listen to what St. Bernard says to him and others like him: "If you have once for all put yourselves in our keeping, why do you take yourselves back again?" (*In Cant.*, sermon. 19). Besides this peace of mind, the obedient man is ennobled and raised above the natural state, since by the sacrifice of his will he has stripped himself of himself, as it were, and put on God, the supreme good, who fills the soul in the proportion in which He finds it emptied of self-will. Thus those who obey from the heart may apply to themselves the words, "I live, now not I, but Christ liveth in me" (Gal. 12:26).[99]

Rome, July 29, 1547. To the scholastics of Gandia. Finally, that obedience is the first condition for the fruit-fulness of our work:

We see by experience that ordinary talents, even those less than ordinary, are very often most effective instruments with a most supernatural efficacy, because they are entirely obedient; and that, by means of obedience, they let themselves be moved and directed by the powerful hand of the Author of all good. On the contrary, we see men of great talent whose work produces no fruit since these men trust in their own management, that is in their self-love, or at least they are not willing to let God our Lord lead them by means of obedience to superiors, and thus the effects which they produce are by no means in proportion to the all-powerful hand of God our Lord, who does not accept these men as His instruments, but are in proportion to the strength of those human hands, which is but weakness and debility.[100]

Rome, December 17, 1552.

To Fr. Miona, provincial of Portugal.

Nevertheless, St. Ignatius intended that the inferior should make courageous use of his own intelligence. Fr. Oliver Manare, when he was appointed rector of Loretto, asked St. Ignatius for some rules of conduct.

"Oliver," *Ignatius replied to him,* "do as seems good to you and as the unction of the Holy Spirit shall teach you. Adapt the rules to the place as well as you can."

And when Manare asked the saint what people he should place in this or that office:

"Tailor the clothes, Oliver, according to the cloth which you have."

One time when he had acted against a written order, Fr. Manare gave Ignatius an account of his reasons. He approved it, saying:

Man gives the order. But God alone gives discernment. In the future I want you to act thus without scruple, according to what you judge the circumstances require, without regard to rules or prescriptions.[101]

At Manresa, when he did not yet have the help of obedience, when he was harassed by scruples which bothered him for months without any confessor being able to help, Ignatius cried out one day in his distress:

Help me, Lord, for I find no remedy among men, nor in any creature. If I thought I could find it, no pain would be too great for me. You show me, Lord, where I may find it. And even if I must follow a little dog for him to give me the remedy, I shall do it.[102]

Chapter VI FAMILIARITY WITH GOD

St. Ignatius roots these three virtues, poverty, chastity and obedience, in the grace of the Holy Spirit which is gained by prayer:

It often happens that the narrow vision of human reasoning does not succeed in perceiving things which a humble recourse to God makes clear to us.[103]

The most important actions, like the most lowly, are to be performed in an atmosphere of prayer. When dealing with the holding of a General Congregation, St. Ignatius writes:

That light by means of which it is possible to decide what decrees should be passed must come down to us from the first and highest Wisdom. Therefore, let Masses be offered and prayers said both in the place of the Congregation and in the other parts of the Society while they are meeting and discussing decrees, to beg grace that all decisions may be made for the greater glory of God.   *Const. VIII, vii, 1.*

It can also happen that, by the help of divine illumination, prayer outstrips reasoning:

If, by a common inspiration and without the formalities of voting, all should acclaim someone, he shall be General.

For the Holy Spirit, who inspires them to this type of election, easily supplies all the orderly formalities of election.

Const. VIII, vi, 5.

All exercises of government shall take place in an atmosphere of prayer:

The first duty of the rector is to sustain the whole college, as it were, on his shoulders by prayer and holy desires.

Const. IV, x, 5.

Each superior should commend that part of the Society which is specially under his care to God by special prayers and by a remembrance in the Sacrifice of the Mass.

Const. IX, vi, 10.

When he had heard the advice of his consultors:

We will sleep on it, *said St. Ignatius.*[104]

It was his way of saying that he would pray over it before making his decision.

Let each personal decision be preceded by prayer:

Subjects should betake themselves to prayer before proposing anything to the superior, and they shall only propose it if, after prayer, they feel it should be done.

Const. III, 2.

Such prayer will sanctify the most profane occupations, such as eating or going to class:

Let grace be said before meals and let thanksgiving follow, and all should say these with fitting devotion and reverence. And while by eating the body is refreshed, let the soul also have her food, by reading some book, pious rather than difficult, which all can understand, and from which they can profit. *Const. III, 1, 5.*

The principal intention of the teachers should be to move the students to the service and love of God. And in order to remind them of this, a short prayer is to be said at the beginning of the class. This prayer is either to be said in such a way that it leads to devotion and edification, or it is not to be said at all. *Const. IV, xvi, 5, C.*

By taste St. Ignatius would have liked the singing of the Office. One day in Holy Week, the feast of St. Joseph, he was in a church to gain the indulgence. He heard the divine

Office chanted and was wonderfully uplifted by the singing:

If I were following my own taste and the inclination of my soul, I would institute the chanting of the Office and choir in the society. But I will not do it because it is not the will of God, and because our institute does not call us in that direction, but in another.[105]

St. Ignatius wished really that his sons' entire lives be so many great prayers:

It is a greater virtue and a greater grace to be able to enjoy our Lord in all sorts of offices and in all sorts of places than in only one. To achieve this we must depend completely on the divine Goodness.[106]

Rome, September 20, 1553. To Francis Borgia.
The most real of prayers is to be ready for all things:

If we direct all things toward God, all things are prayer.[107]

Rome, December 24, 1553. To Fr. Barzee.

Let your soul hold itself tranquil and peaceful, ready to submit to the action of God. Admit divine thoughts generously. Open as wide as possible the gates of your soul.[108]

Rome, September 15, 1548. To Francis Borgia.
But since he knew the numerous easy illusions in which the soul can become involved in a life of prayer, Ignatius always tried to protect his sons from them.

He said that, "of a hundred men who spend their time in long prayers, the greatest number (I do not recall [*says Ribadeneira*], if he said ninety) usually fall into serious deviations from the true path, particularly into obstinacy of mind. This is why he considered that everything depends on mortification and abnegation of will."[109]

He had no confidence in a practice of prayer which was not accompanied by an equal amount of mortification:

When he recommended prayer, he took it for granted that the evil instincts were already under control and mortified, and he referred everything to this.[110]

One day Fr. Louis Gonzáles said of a religious that: "He is a man of great prayer."

He is a man of great mortification, *St. Ignatius corrected him.*[111] *February 23, 1555.*

Then the soul, submissive to God, can follow without fear the call to silence and solitude in which prayer blossoms:

The more our soul finds itself alone and in solitude, the fitter it renders itself to approach and unite itself to the Creator and Lord; and the nearer it thus unites itself to Him, the more it disposes itself to receive graces and favors from His divine and supreme Goodness.   *Ex. p. 10; 20.*

Chapter VII   TO LEAVE GOD FOR GOD

We must not only consider what fervent zeal for the glory of God demands, but also that this zeal should be regulated for the benefit of our neighbor. It will be true zeal, and pleasing to our Lord if it benefits many, and if, looking at God and seeking His glory, I should now and then leave God and thus find Him in our neighbor.[112]

It is not enough to consider God, we must also consider men in the sight of God. In this life we do not only have God our Lord present to witness and to crown our works, but in addition we are a spectacle to angels and to men and to the whole world. Let us strive to do all that is best, not only before God, but before men.[113]

This charity will be the more divine the more universal it is:

The end of our Institute is to take up in the Lord the interests of all people.   *Const. VI, iii, 8.*

Let particular charity never injure the universal, which should always be preferred, since it contributes most to the glory of Jesus Christ our Lord.   *Const. I, iii, 16.*

In the Society there must not be, nor seem to be, any inclination of mind toward either side of any faction which may chance to exist between Catholics; but let there be an universal charity, embracing in our Lord all parties, though at variance among themselves. *Const. X, i, 11.*

Thus when it is known that some men are ill-disposed toward the Society, especially if they be men of great authority, we must pray for them, and use suitable means to make them friendly, or at least not hostile. This should be done, not for fear of contradictions, or because something unpleasant might happen to us, but in order that through the good will of such men, the glory and service of God may grow in all things. *Const. X, i, 11, B.*

Charity will cause the union and the effectiveness of the Society itself:

The chief bond, which will make for union of the members among themselves and with their captain, is the love of God and of our Lord Jesus Christ. If superiors and subjects are very united to the divine and sovereign Bounty, they will very easily have unity among themselves. *Const. VII, 8.*

This union will take place through the same love which descends from God and touches all our neighbors, and, in a special way, the entire body of the Society. And so charity will help in every way toward union, and that which follows charity, a contempt of worldly things by which self-love, the most dangerous enemy of this union and of the common good, is often deceived. *Const. VIII, i, 8.*

Let this charity take precedence over any conflict of opinion:

If there is any difference of opinion, and it seems good to express it, they [the members of the Society] must with modesty and charity advance their reasons with the intention that the truth may appear, and not that they may seem to have the upper hand.[114]

Lest we be deceived, or partisan in our own affairs, it is useful to think of them as if they were the affairs of another, and as if we had to judge of them, not with self-interest and passion, but with truth and reason.[115]

For:

In certain cases, silence is more valuable than speech. It is useless to take up the pen to defend oneself, when the truth defends itself.[116]

Looking upon things in a spirit of faith helps greatly to this charity:

Hence it will follow, that considering one another, they will increase in devotion and praise our Lord God, whom everyone must strive to acknowledge in another as in His image.   *Const. III, i, 4.*

Thus also:

He who is himself evil, easily suspects others. A man who suffers from vertigo believes that the whole world is reeling around.[117]

If they should see one of their brothers fall:

The others must learn from him not to fall themselves, considering that we are all of the same dust, and they must pray God to obtain the effective amendment of their companion who is guilty.[118]

With the greatest sinners, let them act like a mother who exhausts herself with compassion and affection for the sick child. She cares for it and caresses it a thousand times more than if it were strong and healthy.[119]

Among the works of mercy, *wrote Ignatius to Marguerite of Austria,* one, more important than any other, spiritual work of mercy is to console a soul crushed by troubles and sorrows.[120]   *Rome, August 13, 1543.*

To friendship he gave divine overtones:

Between those, *he wrote to the prior of the Carthusians at Cologne,* who are united in our Lord Jesus Christ, by the bond of charity, and by the desire of promoting the honor and the glory of God, there are no letters more sweet than those which the Holy Spirit writes in their hearts by means of their prayers for one another.[121]   *Rome, March 28, 1549.*

To the duke of Gandia, who desired to receive letters from him, St. Ignatius replied:

You ask me not to forget you in my prayers and to come to you through my letters.

89

As far as the first is concerned, I am never lacking there, since I pray for you each day. As to the second, I am convinced that I have satisfied your desire. For I consider that those, who have left themselves to enter into their Creator and Lord, experience a constant attention and consolation in feeling how our eternal Good is present in all things, giving them being and conserving them by His infinite being and presence; and, that for those who love Christ completely, all things help them first of all to gain merit, and to unite themselves in intense love with their Creator and Lord.[122]   *Rome, 1545.*

He prescribed gratitude as a sacred duty to all his sons. On June 14, 1553, he wrote to the entire Society:

Although we must give honor and glory for all good things to God our Creator and Lord, who is the eternal source and beginning of all good, nevertheless we should show to the cooperators and principal ministers of His providence, according to our poor strength, that thankfulness and gratitude which the glory of the divine Majesty demands.[123]

Considered in comparison to the divine Bounty, ingratitude is, of all evils and sins imaginable, one of the things most abominable in the eyes of our Creator and Lord, as well as in the eyes of the creatures which were made for His divine and eternal glory. For ingratitude is a failure to recognize good things, graces, and gifts received.[124]

Rome, March 18, 1542. To Simon Rodríguez.

Chapter VIII THE USE OF HUMAN HANDS

To the scholastics at Coimbra who were preparing themselves for the apostolate through their studies, St. Ignatius wrote:

Another way to help others is to be models of virtue yourselves, so as to make them what you are. In the same way it is the will of the divine Wisdom that the immediate cause used, such as the preacher, or the confessor be himself humble, patient and filled with charity. Wherefore, if you would perfect others, be first perfect yourselves. For though great learning and great virtue are to be sought after, and perfection to be looked for in both, yet to virtue must always be given the preference.[125]   *Rome, May 7, 1547.*

Let them achieve this by:

Seizing all the advantages which help to the greater service of God, and although only the unction of the Holy Spirit and that prudence which the Lord customarily grants to those who have confidence in His divine Majesty are able to teach this, at least a few instructions which may help to dispose the soul for the effects of divine grace should be used to open the way.   *Const. IV, viii, 8.*

Let them attempt to maintain purity of soul and to have a right intention in their studies, seeking nothing else in knowledge than the divine glory and help for souls. They should often in their prayers beg the grace to grow in learning, with this purpose in mind. *Const. IV, vi, 1.*

And even though they may never find any use for the things which they have learned, yet they should be convinced that the work of study, undertaken out of obedience and love, in a work of great merit in the eyes of the divine and supreme Majesty. *Const. IV, 6, 2.*

Let all impediments which could distract the mind from study be removed in order that afterward they may be more useful to others because of the learning which they have acquired. And let all these things be done with a greater desire of serving the divine Majesty. *Const. IV, vi, 3.*

As we must take care lest the love of solid virtue and the religious life grow tepid because of an excessive interest in study, so, at that time, not too much time should be given to mortification, prayers and long meditations. For, in the time of studies, it is even more pleasing to God and our Lord to apply ourselves to learning which is undertaken with a sincere intention of serving God, since the pursuit of learning absorbs almost the whole man. *Const. IV, i, 52.*

They must not study at those times when their health would be injured. Let them give sufficient time to sleep, and let them preserve moderation in the labors of the mind. If this is done, they will be able to persevere longer in them, both in acquiring knowledge and in using it for the glory of God. *Const. IV, iv, 1.*

For health also conditions the work of apostolic ministries. Accordingly, he charged the conscience and the heart of superiors with care of it. To the rector of Alcalá he wrote:

Each one should be treated, as far as possible, in the way which will best help his physical health. We should persuade ourselves in our Lord that the more healthy His servants are, the better they will labor in the business of His divine service.[126] *Rome, June 14, 1554.*

"He was careful that those who wished to enter the society

should have good health and vigorous strength, especially the young. For without these, the coadjutor brothers could not work, nor the students study, nor later work in the service of the Lord. For persons of great learning or prudence he demanded less, since such men, even though but half-alive are still useful." [127]

With a healthy body, *he wrote to Teresa Rejadella*, you can do much work. With a weak body, I do not know what you can do.[128]   *Venice, September 11, 1536.*

As too much solicitude in things appertaining to the body is to be reprehended, so a moderate care of preserving our health and strength of body is praiseworthy, and should be had by all.   *Summary 46.*

Yet when sickness comes, it should be fruitful for the glory of God:

All should labor to draw profit from illness which they should accept as a gift from the hand of our Creator and Lord, seeing it is not less a gift than health. *Const. III, i, 17.*

St. Ignatius had a very unusual charity for the sick. Riba-deneira saw him, when himself sick, leave to Nadal the government of the Society, and still reserve for himself everything which dealt with the care of the sick. He said to Ribadeneira that:

By a wonderful providence of God he had been subject to so many illnesses in order that he could sympathize with the sufferings of others, and be afflicted by their agonies.[129]

For, as it has always been my preoccupation to urge the members of the Society to embrace the most rigid and harsh life, if I had been completely strong in body, and if I had relaxed nothing of the tension of my soul and the austerity of my life, certainly no one would have been able to follow me as I led. But by my weak and broken body God teaches me how to be sick with the sick, and to yield in something to human weakness.[130]

In the Constitutions *he prescribed this rule of supernatural prudence:*

Although there should always be matter for proving virtue and self-abnegation, there should not be lacking the means to sustain nature, and to preserve it for the divine service and praise. *Const. III, ii, 3.*

May He be blessed, *he wrote to Teresa Rejadella,* who has earned for me by His blood eternal health in the participation of His kingdom and His glory. May He give me the grace, so that the good or poor state of my body, and all the rest of His creatures, may always be used for His greater service, praise and glory.[131] *Rome, October 1547.*

He wrote to Isabelle Roser, when she was ill:

I wish you all well-being and all imaginable prosperity which can help you for the glory and the service of God. Yet I think that sickness and other temporal losses often come from the hand of God our Lord so that we may grow in understanding, and renounce the love of created things; and so that we may reflect especially on the shortness of life, in order that, thinking of eternity, we may adorn our souls. Then, thinking that God visits especially those whom He loves, I can feel neither sadness nor pain. I am persuaded that a servant of God, thanks to illness, becomes a doctor more skilled by half in ordering and directing his life to the glory and to the service of our Lord.[132]

Paris, November 10, 1532.

Finally, let death itself be an act of supreme homage to the glory of God:

As in the whole of life, so also and much more in death, every one of the Society must make it his effort and care that God our Lord be glorified and served in him. But since it often happens that the disease is of a kind to hinder greatly the use of the powers of the soul, and since the departure from life is often such that there is need, because of the attacks of Satan, for the aid of fraternal charity, the superior should take care diligently that the one whose life is in danger in the opinion of the doctor be fortified for the transition from temporal to eternal life, before he loses the use of reason, by the reception of the sacraments, as by arms which have been given us by the liberality of Christ our Lord. *Const. VI, iv, 1.*

Chapter IX TO RELY ONLY ON DIVINE MEANS

Trust is a gift of God which He bestows according to His will. We can only obtain it from Him. Normally He gives it only to those who have learned to conquer themselves.[133]

It presupposes perfect detachment from the world:
One who wishes to do great things successfully for the glory of the divine Majesty alone, should guard himself both against the darkness and the light of the world, that is, from foolish fears, smallness of soul, and from the excessively careful plottings of human prudence. Yet we should not act with temerity, nor look for miraculous aid. We should regulate our confidence in God on this certain principle, that His power and His will are not subject to ordinary laws, and that it is not necessary to place our only trust in that which our present strength promises us.

And so when we decide on some business, we should abandon ourselves entirely to God as if success can only come from His hands alone; and at the same time, in the choice and use of means, act as if success could come only from our own labor and industry, insomuch that we should omit nothing which we could do to achieve what we intend.[134]

Thirty years ago, *said Ignatius,* God made me understand that in the matter of His service I should use all means which are fitting and possible, but still put my trust in God and not in those means.[135]

He who is in great fear of the world will never do great things for God. For one can do nothing great for God without the world trying to frighten him by stirring up persecutions and throwing all things into confusion.[136]

For as soon, *he wrote to Isabelle Roser,* as you decide and will to labor with all your strength for the glory, honor and service of God our Lord, by that very fact you join battle with the world and raise a standard against it. You dispose yourself to reject great things by embracing lowly things, no longer considering as of any value greatness or lowliness, honor or dishonor, richness or poverty, love or hatred, welcomes or rebuffs, the fleeting glory, or all the injuries of the times.[137]   *Paris, November 10, 1532.*

It is on that base that our strength should rest. St. Francis Xavier testified that he had learned from St. Ignatius that:

Every son of the Society should make himself conquer and banish the fears which would prevent us from placing our confidence in God alone.[138]

The most solid reasons of faith most abundantly justify that confidence:

One cannot confide too much in Him for whom it is no more difficult to provide than to will.[139]

What would be a miracle would be for God to leave unaided those who trust in Him. Let us occupy ourselves with the service of God, and leave to Him the care of providing for our needs.[140]

In the hands of God I find what is lacking to me in the hands of men. And if they give me nothing, I shall find all things in Him.[141]

Nothing is lacking to the man who possesses God, even though he possesses nothing else; since God is all good and all goods come with God.[142]

St. Peter Canisius has noted this teaching of Ignatius:

Live always in one single atmosphere; be calm in prosperity and in adversity, free from worries in joys or in sorrows.[143]

We must sail against the winds and the storms, and trust in God the more when all things seem lost.[144]

St. Ignatius wished that contradiction should not make us fall back or frighten us:

Let us always push on toward our goal without letting ourselves be hindered by the opposition of our adversaries. We will never lack persecution. If it ever ceases, it will be because we have been wanting in our duty.[145]

To James Miron, provincial of Portugal, who was afraid to take the position of confessor to the king because of the dangers which he would run, St. Ignatius replied:

If we, in our profession, only desire to live in security, and if we wish to give up doing good in order to retreat from danger into shelter, we should neither live nor deal with our neighbor. But according to our vocation, we deal with all men. Even more, as St. Paul says, "I have been everything by turns to everybody to bring everybody salvation" (1 Cor. 9:22). Going on then with a right and pure intention, pursuing, not our interests, but those of Jesus Christ, He himself will protect us by His infinite goodness. And if His powerful hand did not guard this institute, fleeing from perils would not be enough to keep us from falling into graver ones.[146]

Rome, February 1, 1553.

Two sentences sum up his thought:

If anyone forgets himself and his interests for the service of God, God will provide for him better than he could have done, if he had forgotten God to take care of himself.[147]

So then, for the love of our Lord, let us place our hearts entirely in Him, since we owe Him so much. We will more quickly weary of receiving His gifts, than He will of offering them to us.[148]   *December, 1525. To Inez Pascual.*

His followers have delighted in recalling the miraculous effects of this confidence of his.

Fr. Guy Roilet, rector of the German College, was in

97

*extreme poverty. St. Ignatius was struck by his worried air
at Christmas time and asked him:*

"Will the students have something for a little feast on
Christmas?"

"Ah, Father, they scarcely have bread. The baker is un-
willing to give us anything more."

"Well, buy some lamb for them and something for a feast
for the young men and let God take care of it."

*The day after next, Julius III sent to St. Ignatius five
hundred golden crowns which he divided between the
Roman College and the German College.*[149]

Fr. Ribadeneira reports that, among other traits:

In the year 1555 there was at Rome a great scarcity because of a poor harvest and the war which Paul IV was
waging against the kingdom of Naples. The cardinals and
the richest lords were obliged to dismiss a part of their
households since they could not feed them. But God our
Lord provided for those of the Society, who were so numerous, an abundance of everything which was needful to them.
Many saw in this a miracle. One Father, while eating at
Ignatius' table, said, "Yes, certainly this is a miracle."

"What miracle?" *asked St. Ignatius,* "The miracle would
be if it were not so. Since the society has been at Rome, the
more people there are in the house, and the more bitter is
the want in the city, the more abundantly we have received.
Let us serve God. I am sure that He will not abandon us." [150]

The closer one shall bind himself to God, and the more
liberal he shall show himself to His sovereign Majesty, by so
much he shall find God more liberal to him, and be daily
more fit to receive in greater abundance His graces and
spiritual gifts.   *Summary 19.*

Chapter X HE WHO HOLDS THE PLACE OF CHRIST

In the Society of Jesus:

As in all governments and congregations which are well organized, beside those who tend to particular ends, it is necessary that there be someone or even some, who care for the universal good, and who promote it as their proper end, someone who makes this his purpose, the good government, preservation and growth of the whole body of the Society, and this is the General. *Const. IX, i, 1.*

Among the various talents with which according to our desire, the General should be adorned, the first of all is, that in prayer and in all his actions, he be perfectly united in familiarity with God and our Lord. In this way he may obtain more abundantly from Him as from the font of all good an abundant participation in His gifts and graces for the whole Society, and great value and efficacy for all those means which it uses for the help of souls. *Const. IX, ii, 1.*

And especially the splendor of charity toward all, and

99

most of all toward the Society, and the light of a true humility — things which make him pleasing to God and men — these should be easily visible in the General.

Const. IX, ii, 2.

Nevertheless he should have learned to join exactness and the necessary severity with kindness and mercy, so that he will not permit himself to be deterred from that which he judges will be more pleasing to God and our Lord. Yet he should know how to be sympathetic with his sons when it is fitting. He should act in such a way that even those who are reprehended or corrected, though their lower instincts may be displeased, yet will acknowledge that he performs his office exactly in the Lord and with charity.

Const. IX, ii, 4.

He has also much need of greatness and strength of soul to bear the weakness of many, and to carry on great affairs in the service of God, and to persevere in them with constancy when it is necessary, without being cast down by contradictions (even though they come from the mighty and powerful), nor ever letting himself be separated by any prayers or threats of theirs from that which reason and the divine service demand. *Const. IX, ii, 5.*

He should rise above all circumstances which can occur. He should not allow himself to be elated by prosperity, nor cast down by adversity. He should be most ready, if need should arise, to die for the good of the Society, and for the service of Jesus Christ, our Lord and our God.

Const. IX, ii, 5.

He should have unusual talents of mind and will so that he will not be without this ability in the speculative or practical affairs which occur. And, though he who is to be in charge of so many learned men must have learning, prudence is even more necessary, and insight in spiritual and internal things, so that he can discern the action of the good and evil spirit. *Const. IX, ii, 6.*

The most necessary quality requisite for the good conduct of affairs is initiative and energy in beginning them, and intrepid perseverance in bringing them to a successful end, so that they are not left begun but unfinished because of neglect or loss of interest.   *Const. IX, ii, 7.*

As far as the body is concerned, in addition to health, dignity and authority should be considered, and also the bodily strength which his office demands in order that he can fill it for the glory of God and our Lord.

Const. IX, ii, 8.

Finally, the General should be of those who are outstanding for every virtue, who have done good work for the Society, and have been known as such in the Society for a long time. And if any of the above gifts be lacking, certainly there must be trustworthiness, love for the Society, good judgment and suitable learning. As for the rest, many things can be supplied by those who are elected to assist him with the divine aid and favor.   *Const. IX, ii, 10.*

That which has been said for all, namely that they should not be engaged in secular businesses even though they be pious, is much more fitting for the General than for the rest, lest in these or other affairs, even though pious, but not pertaining to the Society, he should allow himself to be so concerned that they deprive him of the time and strength to do those things which are a part of his very office.

Const. IX, vi, 4.

The proper office of the General is not to preach, nor to hear confessions, nor to do other things of this kind, but to govern the whole Society. He will do this, first of all, by his authority, and by the example of his life, and by his charity and by his love of the Society in Christ our Lord, by prayer which is continual and full of desires, and by his Masses which will gain the grace of preserving and increasing the Society. For, of the things which he can do himself, these are the ones which he should consider of greatest import and in which he should have the greatest confidence in the Lord. For by them he is most successful in gaining grace from the divine Majesty from whom come the answers to our prayers.   *Const. IX, vi, 1, 1A.*

By dividing the work with the Provincials in those things which allow of it, and by informing himself of all the more important business, more leisure and time will remain to him to tend to the affairs of the whole Society which he alone can handle. He will thus have more light for understanding what should be done in them than if he wasted a part of his intelligence as happens to those who are unwarrantedly occupied in unimportant details, with the result that the keenness of their intellect becomes blunted therein and incapable of following the important problems.

Const. IX, vi, 6.

Not only does the General need assistants for particular matters, but also for general affairs proper to his office, so that he can settle them more smoothly and well. For it is clear that the memory of one man cannot keep track of so many affairs, and even if it could, the mind of one man would not be sufficient to consider and arrange them all well; and even if he could do this, the strength of one man would not suffice to carry them out.   *Const. IX, vi, 7.*

He needs an assistant who will be his memory and his hands and who, though having no authority, will bear on his shoulders all the burdens of the office.

Const. IX, vi, 8.

So, when the General has these aides, his time should be spent (as far as his health and strength allow), partly with God, partly working with officials and assistants, partly considering things by himself, and deciding courses of action, with the aid and favor of God and our Lord.

Const. IX, vi, 13.

In St. Ignatius the consciousness of authority was joined to a respect for the initiative and responsibilities of his subjects. He wrote to Fr. James Miron, Provincial of Portugal:

It is not the office of the Provincial or of the General to be occupied with the details of business. Even if he possessed all the ability for handling them, it is still better to confide them to others who can then refer what they have done to the Provincial. He will then make whatever decision on the matter his judgment shall dictate.

And if there is a thing which can be left to others, both to deal with and to decide, he will do much better to leave it alone, especially in temporal affairs, and even in many spiritual matters.

As for myself, I act this way, and I find in it not only help and relief, but also more peace and security.

So, as your office demands of you, extend your love toward, and busy your thoughts with the general good of your Province. The measures which are to be taken in this or that affair you should leave to those who, in your opinion, can better take care of them.

When it comes to carrying out decisions, do not involve yourself in it, nor embarrass yourself about it. But rather, as the universal Mover animates and moves individual movers, you will do much more, much better and much more in keeping with your office. If some mistake is made, it is less inconvenient than if you had made it. It is preferable for you to repair the mistakes of your subjects, than that they should correct yours. But this will very often happen, if you engage more than is right in detailed affairs.

May Jesus Christ, God our Lord, grant you the grace in all things to know His will and accomplish it fully![151]

Rome, December 17, 1552.

Fr. Louis Gonzáles has often borne witness to the "liberality" with which St. Ignatius treated subordinate superiors:

It is not good that superiors who have officials under them should wish to interfere too much in their office, treating human beings as instruments by which they work. And for many reasons: 1) because God assists each one with special grace for the charge which is committed to him; 2) because he who sees that the superior wants to do everything himself does not apply himself to his office as much as he could, and as he does when dealing with his own concerns, that is, with love and zeal, so that they will succeed; 3) because experience in the immediate practice of an office sometimes teaches the official things which the superior cannot know by abstract speculation; 4) because often one cannot choose a good course except in accord with the circumstances, and no one who is not in charge can see these; 5) finally because it is much better for the superior to confine himself to correcting his inferiors when they are deficient in their duty, rather than that the inferiors should restrain the superior and give him rules as to one who does not understand what he commands.[152]

The more that subordinate superiors see that you look upon them with confidence, and that they are treated with respect, the more they will willingly enter into the views of their major superiors and work with ardor to do their jobs well, so as not to be surpassed in good will. Actually, when anyone is in charge of a task, he takes more care for its success, he judges better what things will help it, and he receives from heaven appropriate aid to carry it out.

But if the power and the authority are too narrowly limited by superiors, and if they take control of the offices of inferiors, that mistrust is unpleasant, and the zeal of officials slips into that which they have for things which are strange to them; and finally, the grace of heaven is lost.

Further, to do a thing well, a man needs power and competence. But in general he is competent who is in charge and who has the affair constantly before his eyes. If you lessen his power, and if the superior himself, although out of touch with the matter, meddles in the business, power is separated from ability with most inconvenient results. From this arise suspicion, discord, quarrels, when the superiors are not satisfied with their own office, and delve into the offices of others. All order is destroyed by this confusion.[153]

He himself left to subordinates broad powers of initiative.

I recall, says Fr. Louis Gonzáles, *that when he had to give a Father the care of some important business with important people at Rome, he said to him:*

I want you to go and treat of such and such an affair, with this or that cardinal, and I entrust it to you. I desire this or that; these are the means which I think opportune.

Then having given all the information and instruction necessary, he added:

But I want you to use the means which the Lord will show you as more fitting. I leave to you all freedom to do whatever seems better to you.

In the evening, when the Father had returned, Ignatius begin by asking him:

Do you return satisfied? I presume that you have done the business with freedom, and that your decision will be my decision.[154]

"He placed special confidence in subordinate superiors. In 1553 he sent Fr. Miguel de Torres as visitor to Portugal, though he had only been professed a little more than a year. And although there were at that time difficult and important matters to handle, yet he refused to give him rules and regulations for settling and determining things, lest the power and liberty which he wished him to have should be curtailed. He gave him broad general instructions, but no obligation of proceeding in this or that way. He did give him a large number of blank documents signed, so that de Torres could write in them whatever he judged best, as he wished." [155]

St. Ignatius said in the Constitutions:

As the help of grace is more necessary for them on account of the office they hold, so it is to be hoped that God our Lord will grant it to them more generously so that they may think and speak what is most conducive to His glory.

Const. VIII, iii, 2.

As it is the General's task to see that the *Constitutions* of the Society are everywhere observed, so it belongs to him to dispense from them where circumstances demand it, keeping in mind the end of the Constitutions, which is no other but the greater service of God and the good of those who follow this type of life. In all things he should judge according to the mind of those who wrote the Constitutions for the glory of God and our Lord.

Const. IX, iii, 8.

In general, he can command all in virtue of obedience, in anything which is desired to the end proposed by the Society, namely, the perfection and help of the neighbor, for the glory of God. And they must always show him obedience and reverence as one who takes the place of Christ.

Const. IX, iii, 20.

St. Ignatius wants all superiors to exercise their office with kindness and:

To treat inferiors in a way which will give them no just cause for complaint, so that they may be content and serve God with a peaceful mind.[156]

When reprimands are too frequent, they show that he who multiplies them is less moved by zeal for maintaining discipline than by natural impatience; and when they are too severe, this comes from a flaring passion.[157]

A good superior understands that:

It is often his task to supply for the defects of inferior officials and, with the divine favor and help, to bring to perfection that which is not perfect in them. *Const. IX, vi, 2.*

Let the superior:

Use all kindness and modesty and charity in the Lord, as far as he can, so that the subjects can live in love rather than in fear of their superiors. Let him leave something to their free will when it seems to be useful to them. At other times let him show indulgence and sympathize with their weaknesses when there appears to him the more useful course.

Const. VIII, 1, g.

In sum, Ignatius thought as he acted:

He examined the natural inclinations of each with great diligence and watched them carefully, and accommodated himself to them in all things which he considered good.[158]

Superiors who are careful in their office he calls angels. He would say:

The angel of Tivoli, or the angel of Siena.[159]

"When he judged that a severe penance was necessary for some grave fault, he let the guilty man decide what penance was appropriate to his fault. And usually he excused him from a large part of it." [160]

"When there was question of an individual abuse, He did not forbid the thing entirely just to prevent someone from falling, but used an individual remedy." [161]

When people revealed their own faults they were more than pardoned:

"He showed a marvelous love, by covering over and burying in oblivion the faults of those who admitted and exposed them with candor. His restraint and kindness in that matter were incomparable. They could be sure that neither in actions, nor in words, nor in his heart did he keep any more memory of those faults than if he had never known of them." [162]

"When anyone opened his soul to our Father and told him his faults and weaknesses, this seemed to win his heart; and from then on he surrounded that man with a new affection and with a particular care." [163]

He said to Fr. Oliver Manare, when, while Minister at Rome, he was too severe in the case of some novice and invoked "order" as his reason:

Yes, you invoke order, but you neglect charity and discretion.[164]

This same Father, when he became rector of the Roman College, was vexed by his violent temper. Ignatius encouraged him to struggle against it, saying:

A little anger is very helpful for good government, provided that it is moderated by reason and fear of God. It is enough to be careful to restrain it and to repress it so that it does not burst forth. And for the rest, do not be too disturbed by it.[165]

Besides, St. Ignatius loved men of strong character, and bore with those of difficult disposition. To young Edmund Auger, who had a violent temper he repeated:

Conquer yourself, Edmund, conquer yourself, and you will gain a very beautiful crown in heaven.[166]

And he replied to Fr. Manare, who considered this young man unbearable:

More kindly, Father, more softly. For I think that this man, whom you so harshly think worthy of punishment, has made more progress in fervor and mortification in six months, than Juan Cutano and Pedro Canal together in a whole year. *(These were two brothers, "candid, charming, and edifying".)*

To someone who was visiting the house, he showed the street door, saying:

107

This is our only prison. It keeps us from having a prison or people to imprison.[167]

It is by attentive charity that authority will be able to make itself loved:

Since the example of the older Fathers helps much for progress in virtue, inasmuch as the rest are inspired by it to imitate them, the superior, and all the other priests whom he chooses, will for a few days, now and then, during the year take over the tasks of those who serve about the house, so that this type of ministry will be made more pleasing to the others who have been appointed to it for the greater service and glory of God. *Const. III, i, 19.*

He received with great affability and treated with wonderful kindness all subordinates when they came to him. And to know them better, and to give them pleasure, he sometimes had them eat at his table, even the coadjutor brothers, the cook, the porter and those who labored in the most humble offices in the house.[168]

It is in the love of God that the superior finds the strength and the gentleness necessary to bear burdens which seem to him too heavy.

To Manual Sanchez, Bishop of Targo, inquisitor general of Portugal and coadjutor of the Archbishop of Lisbon, who was overwhelmed by his numerous duties, and spoke of resigning, St. Ignatius wrote:

Even if those things which you have undertaken for the divine honor, should not be given up, their weight can be lifted from the soul by not making oneself earthly nor lowly by contact with earthly and lowly things, but by loving them all for God our Lord's sake, and insofar as they are for His greater glory and service. It is our duty to Him who is our last end, and who is in Himself the sovereign and infinite Goodness, to love Him in all things and to let the weight of our love draw us toward Him alone.[169]

Rome, May 18, 1547.

Chapter XI MISSIONARY INSTRUCTIONS

---

*St. Ignatius, when he offered himself and his companions
to the pope, understood that, in the disordered state of
Christianity, the supreme authority of the Church should be
able to send into any part of the world apostles who would
be capable of withstanding evil and promoting the restora-
tion of Christianity.*

*By vow, the professed members of his Society bind them-
selves to accomplish any mission whatsoever which the sovereign pontiff shall impose upon them.*

*In an era when so many reformers were arising on all sides,
and when reform so often only increased the disorder, St.
Ignatius recalled that:*

He, who has the mission, the ability and the desire to
reform the world, should first reform himself, then his fam-
ily; finally let him reform the great capitals of the world.
So his efforts can be crowned with success. Otherwise they
will remain useless.[170]

Let him who wants to be useful to others, make himself
his first concern. Let him be burning with love, if he desires
to set others on fire. Let him conquer all foolish fear. Let

him flee ambition as a deadly disease. Let him give up all forbidden pleasures and all the satisfactions of the flesh. Let him root out of himself every vice, so that, having torn up all the roots of bothersome passions, he may be better disposed to receive the divine seeds within himself and to spread them among others.[171]

"Speaking of some of the Society who, being full of zeal, desired to reform the world, and were meddling in matters of government as if they were politicians, he said that this did not seem good to him. They would do better to think well about the day of judgment when our Lord would ask them for an accounting. For He would not ask them if they had reformed the world, but if they had according, to their institute, heard confessions, preached, taught, directed souls — in brief, if they had helped souls like poor religious."[172]

To undertake great things for the service of the Lord, it is necessary to conquer vain fears, paying no attention to poverty, inconvenience, calumnies, injuries and affronts, nor even to death itself. We should never grow bitter, nor feel hatred nor aversion toward those who contradict or persecute us.[173]

It must be said that very holy men, though they are little able to help others with intellectual talent, he considered very good and very useful. For they make their decisions by consulting God, putting their confidence in Him, and so God enlightens their minds, guides and blesses their work.

Nevertheless, in general, sanctity is not a sufficient qualification for ruling others. Great prudence and judgment are also necessary. Otherwise authority falls into the hands of others who have to make up for this lack of prudence.

But holy men, although they are little qualified to help others by their learning, are very useful, for they preach, even while they are silent, by their example. Just to see them, perhaps, stirs others to truth more successfully than others who have a much greater oratorical ability.[174]

St. Ignatius considered that in such troubled times, it was of the first importance to choose carefully among the tasks which demanded apostolic work. For that reason he sub-

mitted the choice of works to be undertaken to the Holy Father. Then his only task was to obey.

If the Society or the individual apostolic worker has to choose, these are the principles which should govern his choice:

Having before his eyes always as a rule the greater service of God and our universal good, that part of the vast vineyard should be chosen in which there is greater need, both because of the lack of other workers and because of the miserable state of the neighbor; next, the region where the people seem to have the dispositions and willingness so that they can be helped, and then where we have the most obligations.

As good is more divine as it is the more universal, those men and places should be preferred who, when they have been perfected, will be a cause of doing good to many others who follow their authority or are ruled by them.

Const. VII, ii, 1, d.

The members of the Society should first work where spiritual goods are sought, and also where corporal good can be done, in which mercy and charity are exercised. If both together cannot be achieved, the first should be preferred to the second, if all other things are equal.

When some affairs in the divine service are more urgent, others less, the former are to be preferred to the latter.

When some pertain in a particular way to the Society, or when we see that there are no others to undertake them, it is right that the former have the first place in our missions.

When also there are some actions of more universal benefit, which will help more people, as preaching or teaching; others more particular, as hearing confessions or giving the *Spiritual Exercises*, if there is not time for both, the first are to be preferred.

Also, when there are some works which will last longer, and will always bear fruit, others more transient, which will give help rarely or for a short time, it is obvious that the first should be preferred to the second.

Const. VII, ii, 1, c. passim.

Although it be the supreme Providence and the direction of the Holy Spirit which will choose the better part, it can be said in general that in the more important things, where error must be avoided, more carefully chosen men should be sent, in whom greater confidence is placed.

For things which demand greater corporal labors, the stronger and healthier should be sent.

Where there are more spiritual dangers, those who are more tested in virtue and more secure.

Const. VII, ii, 1, f.

Fr. James Miron, Provincial of Portugal, who had refused to be confessor of John III, King of Portugal, invoked for his refusal the reasons which forbid the religious of the Society to accept an episcopate. St. Ignatius recalled what principles should determine his choice:

Certainly I admire your reasons which are founded in humility and prudence. Nevertheless I cannot approve your intention, and I am convinced that you should not continue in that resolution, keeping always before you the greater service of God our Lord: 1) because of our profession which is to administer the sacraments to all classes and all ages of men, to the lowest as to the highest; 2) because of the gratitude we owe to the king; 3) because if you consider the universal good and the greater service of God, there will follow from this assignment great good. For all members share in the well-being of the head.

. . . What you have said of your security does not seem pertinent to me.

Finally as to what people can say, that you seek honors and dignities, this charge will fall of its own weight with the force of the truth and evidence of the facts, when they see that you retain the humility which you have embraced for Christ our Lord.

So, whatever people may say or think, you should not abandon that service of God, and of Their Highnesses, and of the common good.[175]   *Rome, February 1, 1553.*

It is good to:

Begin humbly with the lowest things and to attempt the

highest only if we are called to them; at least as long as circumstances of time, place and person do not invite to the contrary. Rules cannot be formulated for discerning this. The unction of the Holy Spirit will teach it, but the man must have recourse to reflection and diligent observation.[176]

Rome, October 8, 1552. To those sent to the Missions.
Thus he will free himself from illusions:
Do not let the occasions of present good be snatched from your hands, led on by vague hopes of doing greater good in the future. It is a common snare of the devil to swell up our desires, because, in making things which will never happen appear great and full of admirable promise, he turns us from the accomplishment of ordinary things.[177]

To do well that which we do is the first rule of efficiency, for:
No one does more than he who does a single thing. It is especially necessary to observe this rule; it is essential to accommodate ourselves to things, not to accommodate things to ourselves. The latter procedure risks failure because of our unwillingness to inconvenience ourselves.[178]

But we should not:
Be obstinate in continuing a work which we have begun, if there is no hope for its success, or if we judge that we could use our work to better profit at something else.[179]

Nevertheless:
When we have undertaken a good work, let us hold to it without any thought of flight nor of abandoning it shamefully.[180]

To serve the world with negligence and sloth may be pardoned; but to serve God with negligence is something which we cannot permit.[181]

Inconstancy comes from a dangerous temptation of the devil:
We must remain firm in our proper vocation, as if rooted and founded in the house of God; since, as the devil inspires in solitaries the desire of common life, so he makes those who are called to work for the neighbor desire solitude. While pretending to direct us to the service of God, he

guides us to our destruction, by that instability which entices them into ways opposite those in which we should walk.[182]

Fr. Gonzáles remarks that St. Ignatius was very persevering in everything which he undertook. The reasons for this perseverance were:

1) Because he reflected on the undertaking a long while before deciding; 2) because he prayed over it for a long while, and received light from God; 3) because, no matter what it was, he did not act before hearing the advice of those who were well informed about it.[183]

It will also be most important, in order to preserve always the good estate of the Society, diligently to remove ambition, the root of all evils in every state or society. But let each one see in what way he can promote the salvation of souls according to the humility and submission of our profession.

Const. X, 6.

After any one is admitted into the body of the Society in any degree, he must not seek to pass to another, but perfect himself in his own, and employ himself wholly in God's service and glory. *Summary 20.*

Let no one interfere in another's business. *Const. IV, x, 6.*

At the first call of obedience, the apostle will go promptly wherever he is sent:

It is according to our vocation to travel to various places and to live in any part of the world where there is hope of God's greater service and the help of souls.[184]

Summary 3.

The workers of the Society should have only one foot touching earth, the other being always raised to begin a journey.[185]

The missioner should always receive his mission with joyfulness and as from the hand of God.

Const. VII, ii, 1, c.

Purity of heart will make the fruitfulness of his work certain. St. Ignatius often said:

The members of the Society should be like guardian angels to those with whom they deal and who are entrusted to them in two ways, first helping them as much as possible to eternal salvation, second, after they have done all they could, not being disturbed or losing their serenity when the others do not advance.[186]

He who deals with men to gain them for God should be convinced that he is living *in medio nationis pravae.* This should mean that he does not give up helping them because of his horror of the ugliness with which they are often filled. He has undertaken to mold, not gold, but clay. Let him, in his dealing with these sullied souls, be most careful not to stain himself with the same leprosy of which he cleanses them.[187]

No matter what God has deigned to do by their means, let them not therefore consider themselves men of great importance, nor usurp the glory which does not belong to the instrument (which by itself is usually out of all proportion to the effects which it accomplishes, like the jawbone of an ass to destroy the Philistines), but to the arm which directs it.[188]

He alone is strong who relies on the one strength which does not fail:

He who wishes to do great things for God should take care not to be too wise, nor willing to consult only his head and his hands, I mean his limited intelligence and his weak power.[189]

Let them not glory in subtlety of mind, nor ability to speak, nor learning, nor ability in dealing cleverly with others. And let them never think themselves better rewarded, for all which they do for others, than when they receive affronts and injuries, the only recompense which the world pays for truly Christian labors.[190]

In the service of God, we never walk better than when we walk against the wind.[191]

He wrote to his sons, dispersed and persecuted in Europe:

It is no slight grace that the divine Bounty deigns, in letting you taste a gift which should be always the object of our desires, i.e., to be like our guide, Jesus Christ, following our vows and the holy institute of our Society.[192]

Rome, December 24, 1552.

115

The harvest is more bounteous in proportion to the harsh rigor of the preceding winter. And it is a fact that the Society has produced more abundant fruits where Ours have suffered more.[193]

Of all storms, that which we should fear most is the storm of calm. The greatest danger is not to have enemies, but to be without them.[194]

When Fr. Nadal asked St. Ignatius what was the shortest way to achieve perfection, he replied:

Master Nadal, ask God our Lord to give you the grace to suffer much for His love. For to whomsoever He gives this grace, He gives many other graces that are contained in this.[195]

Charity and humility will be the condition of union among the apostles, and also of the honor which they will receive from men:

You shall determine a time each evening to confer on what you have done during the day, and what you should do on the morrow. You will conclude your deliberations by taking a vote, or in some other way. In the morning you will discuss together the course of action for the day.[196]

Rome, March 1546. To Frs. Lainez and Salmeron.

Nothing gives more scandal to seculars than knowing that the religious of the same order are divided among themselves into factions.[197]

To Frs. Lainez and Salmeron, who were sent as papal theologians to the Council of Trent, St. Ignatius wrote:

If I intend to speak and discuss doctrinal questions, it is very useful not to consider my own leisure or lack of time, that is to say, my own convenience. But I should adapt myself to the convenience and leisure of the person with whom I wish to deal, in order to induce him to procure the greater honor of God.[198]   *Rome, March, 1546.*

He who is working to help his neighbor will have more success through humility than through authority, and he will conquer more easily by conforming than by contradicting.[199]

He who speaks of princes or high churchmen or magistrates critically in the pulpit or in public does damage and scandal rather than any good. It is necessary to refrain with great care from this kind of invective.[200]

When a religious loses a temporal thing for the love of God, and to guard peace with his neighbor, God our Lord rewards him abundantly.[201]

Above all, when dealing with some business, lend yourself to that which the business demands and do not demand that it lend itself to you. In other words, do not take account of what suits you, but adapt yourselves to the demands of time and circumstances. In a word, give yourself so well to all, that you become a wise fisher of men to gain all the world, and that, as a servant of Jesus Christ, you act in such a way that you become all things to all men, and that you live only for your brothers in Christ.[202]

To Frs. Salmeron and Broet, when they were sent on a mission to Scotland and Ireland, St. Ignatius recommended: *

In your relations with all, and especially with your equals or inferiors in dignity and authority, speak but little and calmly, listen long and willingly. Listen as long as is required for them to tell you their desires, then reply to them and put an end to the conversation. If they answer in return, cut the discussion as short as possible by a prompt and pleasant dismissal.

In dealing with business, be liberal with time, that is, if you have promised a thing for tomorrow, do it, if possible, today.[203]

Rome, September, 1541.

* St. Ignatius often repeated this advice; the witnesses sometimes give it in a somewhat different form:

You should be more liberal with acts than with words. What you have promised for tomorrow, do today if you can.[204]

If charity and courtesy are not sincere, they are not charity and courtesy, but vanity and cleverness. You should not multiply promises to the point where your actions do not equal your words. So it is not good to promise for tomorrow what you are not able to do successfully today.[205]

If someone asks you to do a thing which you do not think fitting, do not be irritated; refuse firmly, but in such a way that the asker remains sincerely your friend.[206]

THIS IS THE SUM, THIS IS THE SCOPE . . .

The original preface of the Constitutions painted a portrait of the apostle, the soldier of Jesus Christ, a living incarnation of the rules proposed to his sons by St. Ignatius:

Men crucified to the world, and to whom the world itself is crucified, such would the rule of our life have us to be; new men, I say, who have put off their affections to put on Christ; dead to themselves to live to justice; who with St. Paul (2 Cor. 6:5-8) in labors, in watchings, in fastings, in chastity, in knowledge, in long-suffering, in sweetness, in the Holy Spirit, in charity unfeigned, in the word of truth, show themselves ministers of God; and by the armor of justice in the right hand, and on the left by honor and dishonor, by evil report and good report, by good success finally and evil success, press forward with great strides toward their heavenly country.[207]

The Society of Jesus sees always in this exhortation, "the sum and aim of his Constitutions," *the supreme expression of the thought and of the will of Ignatius.*

When Ignatius was sending his sons to the missions, he said farewell to them with the words:

Go, and set the world on fire.[208]

ॐ

ESSAY ON SOURCES

We have attempted to present authentic texts in the form most faithful to the original. They are taken from the *Exercises*, from the *Constitutions* of the Society of Jesus, and finally from the correspondence of St. Ignatius. A few words are necessary to show the relationship between these texts and the life from which they flow.

After living the worldly life of a young nobleman at Court and in the army, Iñigo de Loyola owed to a leg wound he received at Pamplona (1521) the decisive grace of conversion.

The hand of God which had felled him in battle then led him toward the 'folly of the Cross.' The example of St. Dominic and St. Francis aroused his ardor; and so he went to Montserrat, then to Manresa 'dreaming of great things which he should do for the love of God.' These were knightly ambitions which God purified by a long testing. The *Exercises* are the fruit of his own sad experiences, of his anguished search for the will of God. It was thus that he learned the secret of divine prudence. One day this would permit him to guide with well-tested advice those souls who would seek the ways of sanctity. (From 1522 to 1540)

119

Ignatius wrote the *Constitutions* of his Order very slowly. (They were begun in 1544, completed in 1553.)

Between his solitary life at Manresa and the foundation of the Society of Jesus at Rome there passed 15 difficult years, years of pilgrimages, of studies, of many trials, of exaltations which ended, in 1534, with the establishment of a small group of students. On the fifteenth of August of that year they vowed themselves to God. For six years they prayed in obscurity. At last, when events showed them the will of God, at Rome they offered themselves to the Pope as priests, for the service of the Church. It was then that the founder wrote out and submitted basic Formula of the Institute for the approbation of the Apostolic See.

The juridical structure of the Order takes up a large part of the *Constitutions*, but the soul of Ignatius marked with his own spirit and above all with the grace of God his least and his greatest teachings. We will find in the *Constitutions* the practical application of the major doctrines contained in the *Exercises*.

There is also his immense correspondence, continued until his death (1556), with his companions and with innumerable important persons — prelates, princes, religious. You would expect that the cares of government which grew rapidly, occupy the major portion of his letters. Yet the founder, especially in letters to Jesuits dispersed throughout the world, had to transmit the supernatural wisdom which governed their apostolic action. In this case the doctrine of the *Exercises* and the principles of the *Constitutions* take on a precise form for particular situations. In the letters will be found expressions, exact, flexible, concrete, considerate of men and of circumstances. In such expressions wisdom, inspired by love, assumes the form most capable of touching men and enlightening them.

There are also numerous testimonies gathered by oral tradition which are too interesting to be neglected.

These words of St. Ignatius are reported to us by his familiar disciples, the first companions, or at least by witnesses of the first generation of the Society of Jesus. Among them the following especially should be heard: Peter Ribadeneira, Luis Gonzáles, and Oliver Manareus.

P. Ribadeneira, a novice very dear to Ignatius, lived in close connection with him at Rome. He wrote in Spanish and in Latin a very full *life*. The edition we have used in this translation is: *Vida del Bienventurado Padre Ignacio de Loyola, Fundador de la Religion de la Compania de Jesus,* por el Padre Pedro de Ribadeneira, religioso de la misma Compania, Segunda Edicion, Barcelona, Imp. y Libreria de la Viude e Hijos de J. Subirana, 1885. (cited in the footnotes as "Ribad.") He himself says that he wrote his work from his personal memories, from the oral and written witness of P. Lainez and from the work of P. Luis Gonzáles.

Luis Gonzáles about 1553 gathered from the lips of Ignatius those memoirs which he had finally consented to confide to him after many requests from his advisers. Gonzáles took random notes which he then dictated in Spanish or in Italian. Of them he constructed a narrative which he brought up to the time when Ignatius wrote down the *Constitutions*. This narrative was translated into Latin by P. Hannibal Codretti. The complete text is contained in the *Acta Sanctorum,* of the *Bollandists,* the 31 July, p. 634–654, under the title, *Acts of Father Ignatius*. A French translation has been published entitled: *Le Récit du Pélerim* by P. Thibaud, Louvain, 1922. We quote from the *Monumenta Ignatiana,* (Series 4) "Scripta de S. Ignatio," Tomus Primus, Matriti (Madrid), Typis Gabrielis Lopez del Horno, 1904. (cited in the footnotes as "Scrip.")

Still more directly, those two disciples have given us extremely precious testimony which preceded the redactions which they made from it and published. This consists in the *Journal,* or *Memorial* of P. Luis Gonzáles, noted down without any fixed order. It is edited in the *Monumenta (ibid).* Secondly it consists in the early collection noted by P. Ribadeneira: *De Actis P.N. Ignatii;* then in a revision of this: *Dichos y Hechos de N.P. Ignacio;* finally in a little notebook: *De el gobernio de N.P. Ignacio.* These are all contained in the same volume of the *Monumenta.*

Finally we should note the Reply of P. Oliver Manareus to the questions which were proposed to him by P. Lancisius. (*Monumenta, ibid.*)

The testimony of P. Lainez, the collection of P. Lancisius add little to the work of their predecessors.

Further, we have included some testimony from later accounts which we found particularly interesting. These are:

Della Vita e dell'Istituto de S. Ignazio, Fundatore della Compagnia di Gesù, by Daniele Bartoli, Florence, Presso Leonardo Ciardetti, 1831. (cited in the footnotes as "Bartoli".) Books III and IV collect the spiritual teachings of St. Ignatius.

Compendio della Vita di S. Ignatio di Loiola, by Vigilio Nolarci, Venice, 1680. Its last chapter (48th) contains numerous sayings of Ignatius.

* *S. Ignatii Apophtegmata*, by P. Hadrianus Lyraeus, Anvers, 1682.

* *Liber Sententiarum Sancti Ignatii Loyolae*, Bononiae, 1804, in the appendix to an edition of the letters of St. Ignatius by P. Roch Menchaca. This book contains 443 sentences of which the author unfortunately omits the sources. We can attest that the editor, a learned man of great probity, has made a very serious choice which we have often verified. His witness should be retained.

Use has been made also of *De Vita et Moribus S. Ignatii Loyolae*, by John Peter Maffeius, S.J., Libri III, Verona, in Nova Typog. Petri Ant. Berni, 1719.

It is clear that these various witnesses, the last especially, give to the words of St. Ignatius a revised form which is not the original. Sometimes they report them indirectly, sometimes directly. We have tried to show the differences in form and quality of these citations by typographical changes.

The reader who desires to obtain a precise knowledge of the person and work of Ignatius can have recourse to such texts and studies as the following:

St. Ignatius of Loyola, by Paul Dudon, S.J., translated by

William J. Young, S.J. Milwaukee, Bruce Publishing Co., 1949.

There is a brief and penetrating biography by Fr. C.C. Martindale, S.J.

There is an English edition of the *Text of the Spiritual Exercises of St. Ignatius*, published by the Newman Bookshop, Westminster, Md., 1943.

St. Ignatius Loyola, The Pilgrimers, by James Brodrick, S.J., New York, Farrar, Straus and Cudahy Co., 1956.

On the spirituality of St. Ignatius see the following:

The Ignatian Way to God, by A. Brou, S.J., translated by William J. Young, S.J., Milwaukee, Bruce Publishing Co., 1952.

Ignatian Methods of Prayer, translated by William J. Young, S.J., Milwaukee, Bruce Publishing Co., 1949.

Contemplation In Action: A Study In Ignatian Prayer, by Joseph Conwell, S.J., Spokane, Gonzaga University Press, 1957.

Finding God In All Things: Essays In Ignatian Spirituality, selected from *Christus*, translated by William J. Young, S.J., Chicago, Henry Regnery Co., 1958.

St. Ignatius' Own Story, translated by William J. Young, S.J., Chicago, Henry Regnery Co., 1956.

An Ignatian Approach To Divine Union, by Louis Peeters, S.J., translated by H. L. Brozowski, S.J., Milwaukee, Bruce Publishing Co., 1956.

A Letter On Obedience, translated by William J. Young, S.J., New York, The America Press, 1953.

La Spiritualité de la Compagnie de Jésus, by Joseph de Guybert, S.J., Rome, Bibliotheca Instituti Historici, S.J., 1953.

The *Constitutions* exist only in Latin. There is a work by P. P. de Chastonay, *Les Constitutions de L'ordre des Jesuites*, which shows the place of the work of St. Ignatius, Editions Montaigne, Paris.

The Letters form twelve volumes of the *Monumenta Ignatiana*. They are cited in the footnotes as "*Epist.*"

All references contained in the notes except the few noted have been verified by the translator in the earliest edition of the work available to him. These editions are the ones cited above. The works of the authors marked with an asterisk were not available to the translator, and so he has copied the author's footnote as it stood. Wherever the translation differs from the French, it does so in an effort to render more accurately the original Spanish or Italian.

NOTES

[1] Bartoli, IV, 37, p. 181.
[2] *Epist.* I, p. 95.
[3] M.I., *Const.* I, p. 133.
[4] *Scrip.* p. 54, 55.
[5] *Scrip.* p. 403.
[6] M.I., *Const.* I, p. 113, 128.
[7] *Scrip.* p. 399.
[8] *Scrip.* p. 49.
[9] M.I., *Const.* I, p. 111.
[10] Ribad. I, ii, p. 25.
[11] *Scrip.* p. 32.
[12] Ribad. V, ii, p. 501.
[13] Ribad. V, i, p. 482.
[14] Bartoli, IV, 19, p. 92.
[15] *Epist.* I, p. 80.
[16] *Epist.* I, p. 408.
[17] Bartoli, I, 35, p. 200.
[18] *Epist.* I, p. 296–297.
[19] Ribad. V, x, p. 595.
[20] Bartoli, IV, 37, p. 183.
[21] *Scrip.* p. 491.
[22] *Epist.* I, p. 72.
[23] *Epist.* II, p. 233–234.
[24] *Epist.* III, p. 510.
[25] *Epist.* I, p. 501.
[26] *Epist.* I, p. 113.
[27] Bartoli, IV, 37, p. 177.
[28] *Epist.* I, 255.
[29] *Epist.* I, p. 146.
[30] *Epist.* I, p. 498.
[31] *Epist.* I, p. 79–80.
[32] Bartoli, IV, 4, p. 18.
[33] *Scrip.* p. 395.
[34] Wolarci, *Vita*, c. 32, p. 417.
[35] *Scrip.* p. 399.
[36] *Epist.* I, p. 72.
[37] Lyraeus, I, Apo. 5.
[38] Bartoli, III, 12, p. 50.
[39] Menchaca, 124.
[40] *Epist.* I, p. 506.
[41] *Epist.* II, p. 234.
[42] Menchaca, 316.
[43] *Epist.* I, p. 84–87.
[44] *Epist.* I, p. 502.
[45] Ribad. V, i, p. 481.
[46] *Epist.* I, p. 109.
[47] *Epist.* VI, p. 223.
[48] *Epist.* I, p. 109.

[49] *Epist.* I, p. 497.
[50] Bartoli, IV, 26, p. 120.
[51] *Epist.* I, p. 80.
[52] Bartoli, I, 35, p. 201.
[53] *Scrip.* p. 78.
[54] Wolarci, *Vita*, c. 48, p. 627.
[55] Bartoli, IV, 37, p. 179.
[56] *Epist.* I, p. 81.
[57] Bartoli, III, 1, p. 6.
[58] Bartoli, III, 1, p. 6.
[59] Wolarci, *Vita*, c. 27, p. 357.
[60] Ribad. V, i, p. 481.
[61] *Epist.* I, p. 504.
[62] *Epist.* I, p. 103.
[63] *Epist.* I, p. 98.
[64] Ribad. V, x, p. 586–587.
[65] Bartoli, IV, 37, p. 189.
[66] *Scrip.* p. 200.
[67] *Epist.* I, p. 82.
[68] Ribad. III, x, p. 579.
[69] Ribad. III, xv, p. 277.
[70] *Epist.* I, p. 139.
[71] *Epist.* I, p. 451.
[72] *Examen Generale*, IV, 44; M.I. Series 3, *Const.* III, p. 28.
[73] *Epist.* I, p. 499.
[74] *Scrip.* p. 244.
[75] Lyraeus, II, Apo. 2; Menchaca, 113.
[76] Bartoli, IV, 27, p. 178.
[77] *Epist.* I, p. 81.
[78] *Epist.* I, p. 95.
[79] *Epist.* I, p. 81.
[80] Bartoli, III, 38, p. 157.
[81] Ribad. V, iii, p. 504.
[82] *Scrip.* p. 298.
[83] Bartoli, III, 1, p. 8.
[84] *Scrip.* p. 470.
[85] M.I., *Const.* I, p. 131.
[86] Bartoli, IV, 37, p. 182.
[87] *Epist.* III, p. 303.
[88] Ribad. V, i, p. 487.
[89] *Epist.* IV, p. 671.
[90] Ribad. V, iv, p. 513.
[91] *Epist.* IV, p. 671.
[92] Wolarci, *Vita*, c. 30, p. 386.
[93] *Epist.* IV, p. 675.
[94] *Scrip.* p. 433.
[95] *Epist.* IV, p. 676.
[96] *Epist.* IV, p. 679.

[97] Bartoli, III, 24, p. 104.
[98] Bartoli, III, 24, p. 104.
[99] *Epist.* I, p. 554, 556.
[100] *Epist.* IV, p. 561.
[101] *Scrip.* p. 519.
[102] *Scrip.* p. 51.
[103] Bartoli, IV, 37, p. 187.
[104] *Scrip.* p. 234.
[105] *Scrip.* p. 348.
[106] *Epist.* II, p. 234.
[107] *Epist.* VI, p. 91.
[108] *Epist.* II, p. 234.
[109] *Scrip.* p. 432.
[110] *Scrip.* p. 367.
[111] *Scrip.* p. 367.
[112] Ribad. V, x, p. 589.
[113] Ribad. V, x, p. 588.
[114] Bartoli, III, 1, p. 7.
[115] Bartoli, IV, 37, p. 187.
[116] Ribad. IV, 12. (this reference could not be verified)
[117] Menchaca, 297.
[118] Bartoli, III, 1, p. 8.
[119] Bartoli, IV, 20, p. 97.
[120] *Epist.* I, p. 272.
[121] *Epist.* II, p. 368–369.
[122] *Epist.* I, p. 339.
[123] *Epist.* V, p. 126.
[124] *Epist.* I, p. 192.
[125] *Epist.* I, p. 508.
[126] *Epist.* VII, p. 108.
[127] *Scrip.* p. 445.
[128] *Epist.* I, p. 108.
[129] *Scrip.* p. 368.
[130] *Scrip.* p. 368.
[131] *Epist.* I, p. 628.
[132] *Epist.* I, p. 84.
[133] Bartoli, IV, 36 (this reference could not be verified)
[134] Bartoli, IV, 37, p. 175.
[135] *Scrip.* p. 391.
[136] Bartoli, IV, 37, p. 176.
[137] *Epist.* I, p. 86.
[138] Bartoli, IV, 22, p. 108.
[139] Bartoli, IV, 23, p. 112.
[140] Bartoli, IV, 23, p. 110.
[141] Bartoli, IV, 23, p. 109.
[142] Bartoli, IV, 37, p. 178.
[143] Menchaca, 424.
[144] Bartoli, IV, 23, p. 108.

[145] Bartoli, IV, 37, p. 176.
[146] *Epist.* IV, p. 627.
[147] Bartoli, IV, 37, p. 175.
[148] *Epist.* I, p. 72.
[149] *Scrip.* p. 522.
[150] *Scrip.* p. 369, 372.
[151] *Epist.* IV, p. 558.
[152] Bartoli, IV, 37, p. 198.
[153] Maffei, p. 313–314.
[154] *Scrip.* p. 284.
[155] *Scrip.* p. 284.
[156] Ribad. V, vii, p. 554?
[157] Bartoli, III, 36, p. 150.
[158] Ribad. V, vii, p. 557.
[159] *Scrip.* p. 524.
[160] *Scrip.* p. 453.
[161] *Scrip.* p. 476.
[162] *Scrip.* p. 451.
[163] *Scrip.* p. 436.
[164] Wolarci, *Vita*, c. 28, p. 373.
[165] *Scrip.* p. 514.
[166] Ribad. V, x, p. 579.
[167] Wolarci, *Vita*, c. 31, p. 396.
[168] *Scrip.* p. 449.
[169] *Epist.* I, p. 514.
[170] Lyraeus, II, Apo. 15.
[171] Ribad. V, xi, p. 601.
[172] *Scrip.* p. 435.
[173] *Scrip.* p. 459–460.
[174] Bartoli, IV, 37, p. 196.
[175] *Epist.* IV, p. 626.
[176] *Epist.* XII, p. 252–253.
[177] Bartoli, III, 1, p. 8.

[178] Bartoli, IV, 37, p. 176.
[179] *Scrip.* p. 463.
[180] Bartoli, IV, 19, p. 92?
[181] *Scrip.* p. 470.
[182] Bartoli, III, 1, p. 8.
[183] *Scrip.* p. 293.
[184] *Examen Generale* IV, 35; M.I.
Series 3, *Const.* III, p. 26.
[185] Lyraeus, II, Apo. 14, p. 188.
[186] *Scrip.* p. 515.
[187] Bartoli, IV, 37, p. 197.
[188] Bartoli, III, 1, p. 7.
[189] Bartoli, IV, 22, p. 107.
[190] Bartoli, III, 1, p. 7.
[191] Bartoli, III, 35, p. 148.
[192] *Epist.* IV, p. 564.
[193] Bartoli, II, 18, p. 88.
[194] Bartoli, II, 18, p. 88.
[195] Ribad. V, x, p. 595.
[196] *Epist.* I, p. 387, 389.
[197] *Scrip.* p. 469.
[198] *Epist.* I, p. 387.
[199] Bartoli, IV, 37, p. 191.
[200] Lyraeus, III, Apo. 6, p. 397.
[201] *Scrip.* p. 470.
[202] Ribad. V, xi, p. 605–606.
[203] *Epist.* I, 179, 180.
[204] Ribad. V, xi, p. 603–604.
[205] Bartoli, IV, 37, p. 185.
[206] Ribad, V, xi, p. 604.
[207] M.I.,*Const.* III, p. CXLIX.
[208] Bartoli, IV, 14, p. 61.